An Anthology of Piano Music Volume III

The Romantic Period

**Selected and Edited
by Denes Agay**

**With an Introduction
by Louis L. Crowder**

Head of the Department of Music
The University of Connecticut

Yorktown Music Press: New York
Music Sales Limited: London

Library of Congress Catalog Card Number: 72-150252
ISBN: Hardcover Edition
       Complete Set: 0-8256-8049-2
       Volume III: 0-8256-8047-6
ISBN: Softcover Edition
       Complete Set: 0-8256-8040-9
       Volume III: 0-8256-8043-3

FOREWORD

The content of AN ANTHOLOGY OF PIANO MUSIC was selected from the keyboard literature of nearly four centuries. From the early Baroque to the present, through the works of 139 composers, all important musical idioms and modes of expression are represented. The material is divided into four volumes:

Volume I —THE BAROQUE PERIOD— from the end of the 16th century
(late Renaissance) to the end of the 18th (Rococo).

Volume II —THE CLASSICAL PERIOD— the second half of the 18th
and the early 19th centuries. (Haydn, Mozart, Beethoven
and their contemporaries.)

Volume III—THE ROMANTIC PERIOD— piano music of the 19th century.

Volume IV—THE TWENTIETH CENTURY— piano works by major composers
of our time.

It is hardly necessary to point out that no rigid stylistic boundaries separate these volumes and that, inevitably, there is some chronological and idiomatic overlapping. The works of the sons of Johann Sebastian Bach, for instance, which conclude the baroque volume could have been placed as well at the beginning of the classical section. Fauré, Sibelius, Rachmaninoff and others, who wrote during the late 19th and early 20th centuries, could have been included in either the romantic or the contemporary volume, depending on whether we consider their modes of writing or their life-spans as a yardstick. It is better, then, to view this Anthology, and for that matter, the entire music literature, not as a succession of clearly separated and defined plateaus, but rather as a broad, ever-flowing stream with many branches and tributaries. This stream, the literature of keyboard music, is so vast that even the impressively sizable body of this Anthology, amounting to nearly one thousand pages, can represent but a small fraction of it.

This fact alone can give a hint of the difficult process involved in selecting the contents of these volumes and of the often thorny decisions the editor had to make. Which Preludes and Fugues of Bach's "48" should be chosen? Which Sonatas of Mozart and Beethoven should be included? Are the contributions to keyboard romanticism of an Heller or an Alkan substantial enough to warrant inclusion? Is the amount of space allocated to a certain composer in proper ratio to his importance? These and other similar questions had to be answered, always keeping in mind the main purpose of this Anthology and constantly trying to achieve a reasonable balance between the aesthetic, pedagogic, and historic considerations on the one hand and the dictates of space limitations on the other.

The purpose of this Anthology is twofold: to present a comprehensive survey of the entire keyboard literature through works which are appealing and representative, without being too demanding from either a musical or technical point of view; and to furnish an academically sound and varied teaching and performing library. The grade level of the contents ranges from easy to advanced, with the bulk of the material falling well within the intermediate grades. We felt that this segment of the piano repertory can furnish the most suitable materials for our multi-purpose collections. For this reason, works demanding utmost musical maturity and technical virtuosity, such as the late Sonatas of Beethoven, the lengthier concert pieces of Schumann, Chopin, Liszt, and others were not included.

All selections are based on authentic sources and are in their original forms. Tempo, dynamic, and expression marks in small print or in parentheses are editorial additions and should be regarded as suggestions rather than rigid directions. In line with our aim to give the player an authentic as well as a practical edition, the less familiar ornamental signs, especially those of the English virginalists and the French clavecinists, were replaced by the equivalent and better known symbols of the German Baroque (J. S. Bach). There is a review of these ornamental signs and their execution on page 18 of our baroque volume. To aid the performer in avoiding the often puzzling problems involved in the recognition and correct interpretation of *long appoggiaturas,* these signs have been written out in conventional notation throughout the baroque and classical volumes.

The main body of this Anthology is compiled from the music of the great masters. Included are not only their well-known repertory pieces, but also other of their representative works which are seldom found in similar collections. We have also included a number of relatively unknown, nonetheless delightful pieces by a few minor masters. These composers were perhaps not creative minds of the first magnitude but they did produce occasional works of striking beauty, especially in the smaller forms, and should be entitled to the measure of recognition offered by an anthology.

We hope to have succeeded in conveying the many factors, viewpoints and considerations which guided the selection of materials for these volumes. The final choices inevitably reflect, of course, the personal taste and didactic principles of the editor. It should be noted, however, that the process of compilation also included extensive consultations and discussions with many distinguished pianists and educators. To them, too numerous for individual mention, we express our heartfelt thanks and gratitude. In addition, we are deeply indebted to Mr. Eugene Weintraub, for his invaluable editorial help, to Mr. Herbert H. Wise, for his patience and wisdom in guiding this large publication project, and to Professor Louis L. Crowder, for his richly illuminating commentaries on the styles and performance practices of each period.

October 1970   DENES AGAY

CONTENTS

THE ROMANTIC PERIOD by Louis L. Crowder

Romanticism, with perverse disregard for the orderly compartmentalizing of music history, did not appear miraculously in the 1830's, romantic though that would have been, at the first trumpet blast manifesto of Schumann's David Society. Its roots ran deep and far, paradoxically back to the heyday of Classicism and even before. It is significant that the romantic movement in music, aside from encouragement from certain individuals in Paris, was almost entirely a German phenomenon. In fact it could have been predicted almost to the decade on the evidence of the strangely sentimental, unrestrained emotional orgy that occurred throughout Germany after 1750. Involved were *Pietism,* a popular religious reaction against stern Lutheran theology; the *Empfindsamkeit* (Sensitiveness) period in music, C. P. E. Bach and the Mannheim School; the *Sturm und Drang* (Storm and Drive) of the 1770's, a youthful literary movement stressing the revolt of the individual. All left a heavy imprint on the composer of the classical period, and all were evidences of a basically romantic inclination in German society.

C. P. E. Bach's Fantasias without bar lines, for example, and his dramatic accents and shifts from tenderness to violence, as well as many of Haydn's early works, with their asymmetric phrase structures, their pathos and sentimentality, all have unmistakeable touches of both "Empfindsamkeit" and "Sturm und Drang." In spite of a leap-frog chronology that vaulted several decades, these indications pointed directly to the romantic nineteenth century.

The motivation for the romantic movement lay in the changing state of mind of intellectual Europe, and in the resulting changes in social institutions. The thoughts of Rousseau, particularly his belief in the essential goodness of man, and his distrust of Reason, pervaded the era. The explosion of the French Revolution had begun, a generation earlier, the emancipation of the individual; its booming reverberations still ricochetted from one court to the other and would continue to be heard throughout the nineteenth century. Absolute regimes still lingered on in many small German states, but neither rulers nor ruled believed in their divine origin. The individual became, for the first time in the history of the arts, more important than the society in which he lived. Ultimately he helped transform that society.

Freedom And Music

Political freedom implied and abetted artistic freedom, particularly the freedom to express personal feelings on the most intimate levels and through the widest possible range, without the artist's even giving thought to the complicated restraining etiquettes of Classicism. This new esthetic ideal, foreshadowed as we have seen in the eighteenth century, burst into full bloom in the nineteenth, with incalculable results for music. Here for once we have, in early Romanticism, an era approaching unanimity in its ideas on the nature of music, its purposes, and the methods for achieving them. Since each composer was his own heroic ideal, the products of this common purpose were exceedingly diverse, but all reflected the basic tenet of Romanticism: to express oneself at all costs.

Freedom in the use of one's emotional state as the material of composition necessarily led to new attitudes toward composition itself—new techniques, new forms, and particularly new sonorities. All these will be touched upon later. In the meantime how did Romanticism, with the stage set for its entrance, manage to appear?

Actually it was long overdue. The powdered wig was gone. The biting wit and inexorable logic of Voltaire were obscured by the mists of emotion, which now inspired the same complete confidence accorded a half century earlier to Reason. The princelings were tottering, before long many would be eliminated and others reduced to ineffectuality. It was a heady era, ripe for revolution.

Perhaps it only awaited the combined efforts of a few men of genius and courage to make aspiration a reality. It was a happy coincidence that the greatest of the early Romantics, the guiding spirits of the entire movement, were born within a period of three years, Mendelssohn in 1809, Chopin and Schumann in 1810, Liszt in 1811. All shared the intoxication of their time and were part of the ferment that produced Romanticism. Certainly no more remarkable and deliberate reshaping of musical values has ever occurred. In paraphrase of Schumann's salute to Chopin, "Hats off, gentlemen, a genius," we may say with fuller justice, "Hats off, musicians, the most remarkable assemblage of geniuses ever seen."

The actual emergence of the great romantic composers was the result of a hard-fought battle against mediocrity. Led by Schumann, the younger modernists probably accelerated by fifty years a process that may have been inevitable, but which was strengthened by their revolutionary fervor. Indeed some of the most inspiring pages of music history were written, literally, by Schumann himself, who through his critical attacks on the shallow virtuosity of his day and his championing of the emerging young romantic composers, actually reversed within his lifetime the effects of a debased public taste.

From our vantage point it seems regrettable that a conflict was necessary, but the sorry fact is that the public of the mid-nineteenth century was neither worthy, nor even aware, of its great composers. The names which figured most prominently on concert programs of the 1840's are now forgotten even by musicians, Döhler, Herz, Hünten, Kalkbrenner and others representative of the shallow exhibitionism that for a time all but eclipsed the pure flame of Chopin, Schumann, and Mendelssohn.

The Varying Fortunes Of Romanticism

The last half of the century, however, was nothing short of a triumphal march for Romanticism. No one doubted that music had at last reached the very pinnacle of sophistication and artistic validity. Previous eras, when they were noticed at all, were usually patronized as interesting antiques. Wagner was to be the Music of the Future, and all was well. The only misfortune was that once music had reached this dizzying height in its evolution, there was nowhere else to go, or so it was believed until 1900.

Regrettably, but understandably, the first fifty years of the twentieth century were deliberately unkind to the nineteenth. Romanticism's overt expression of strong or intimate personal emotion seemed to many, during the 1920's and 30's, more remote in spirit than the "cooler" eighteenth century. As a result the twentieth century tended to avoid musical involvement on the personal level. Neo-classicism flourished along with a revival of interest in polyphony, both anti-romantic influences. There has in fact persisted to the present day a somewhat cerebral flavor in much recent composition, whatever its professed philosophy.

At least this has been true with "serious" music; on other levels there has never been a scarcity of romanticism. Popular music has always been nourished on a romantic diet, in its crudest form no doubt, but romantic none the less. And though Jazz was often "classic," Blues was not. In most "rock," all "soul" music, and in most popular songs, at least in the words, romance flourishes unchallenged. In reality only a sophisticated minority of the musical community indulged in sneers at romanticism, and one senses some artificiality in their condescension. Most of us cherish a persistent streak of romanticism regardless of the "spirit of our time," although one must admit that there was a period when many musicians seemed reluctant to admit it.

Perhaps there were reasons, beyond the natural aversion of one century for its predecessor, for this cyclic decline in "official" respect for romanticism. Obviously a protracted era like the Romantic must progress within itself. Beethoven could not be repeated, he had to lead to the young Romantics. And after they had explored the intimacies of the human psyche and had given us works of incomparable beauty and insight, they could only be followed by Wagner and Brahms. Thereafter few choices remained. One led to the disintegration of tonality and with it of Romanticism itself, to be reborn after 1900 in the still-romantic twelve-tone cosmos of Schönberg's Vienna. Another line of evolution accomplished a complete reversal of the premises of German Romanticism and brought forth Debussy's new French Romanticism, which in turn led to the various byways of much contemporary music. As a third and last alternative, the persistently romantic bias of some composers produced a tenacious late-romanticism on traditional premises. Unfortunately most of these late-blooming flowers on the romantic vine were doomed to wither and degenerate through emotional exaggeration, a process spilling well over into the twentieth century. These late excesses may be partially to blame for the decline of the reputation of Romanticism that took place fifty years ago.

This decline is not reflected today in any public disfavor. Romantic music is enjoying revival on a spectacular scale. For example, whereas thirty years ago many a young pianist considered the Tchaikovsky Concerto blatantly sentimental, it has enjoyed a vigorous resurrection. And who shall say that it shouldn't? Like other late-romantic works, it is a sincere communication from a dedicated musician, who is not to be blamed for not being Beethoven. More important, this music gives pleasure to millions, some of whom are on the way to enjoying Mozart or Schubert. So let us praise its virtues, overlook its faults, and even shed a tear or two at the proper moments. But let us not forget that it does not wholly typify the romantic movement, which includes, after all, some of the greatest composers in history. We shall no doubt continue to turn to them for musical solace not to be found in the music of any other period.

Romanticism And The Piano

The high tide of Romanticism, as far as piano music is concerned, occurred in the works of Chopin, Schumann and Liszt. Schumann, the more original, Chopin, the more skillful, and Liszt, the more theatrical, helped create a literature for the piano far richer than that of any other instrument. Who among the string or woodwind players has inherited such mountainous resources? And such a wealth of pieces for every degree of advancement, from the very easy to the most difficult! Though the baroque and the classic eras both contributed enormously to keyboard music, by far the largest windfall came from the Romanticists, some of whom, like Chopin and Schumann, wrote very little else as important as their piano works.

The emergence of the modern piano in the early 1800's accounts for this. Just at the time when the individual and his feelings and needs became the concern of philosophers, of the arts, and of politics (remember how many revolutions there were in Europe in the 1800's) there developed from modest classical beginnings an instrument ideally suited to a type of music that could express these feelings and fill these needs; one person alone, independent of accompanist or ensemble, with the world of great piano music at his fingertips!

Expressive resources were of course at hand for the harpsichordist of the baroque or for the pianist of the classical period, but the extent of these resources pales beside the wealth of those offered by the century of the piano. For in many ways, notwithstanding the great things that were created in other media, we are justified in thinking of the nineteenth century as indeed the century of the piano. In spite of its abuse by virtuosi and charlatans, it filled the most vital need of its time. With it the solitary individual could, for the first time in history, fulfill his artistic needs and express his innermost feelings, no matter what their range. Professional pianists multiplied by hundreds, amateurs by thousands, and soon the home without a piano, and at least one family member to play it, was no home at all. Conservatories appeared all over Europe, largely to meet this demand, and the publishing business throve as never before.

Thanks largely to this remarkable upsurge in the piano's popularity, it continues to flourish today, in spite of all the things that have revolutionized musical life in the past fifty years. The fact is that once accustomed to the piano we can't get along without it, which is another way of saying that we still need Romanticism. This is probably because human feeling has not changed appreciably since pre-history. In the cave paintings of Lascaux we share the emotional experience of Cro-magnon man of more than 20,000 years ago. We are moved by Homer, by Shakespeare, by Nefertiti or by the Nike of Samothrace. Time has nothing to do with it. We are all at heart both Classicists and Romantics. But I suspect that although we might manage for a time without Classicism, we could not survive spiritually for very long without at least some music of the romantic period.

Romantic Music And Music Study

None of us is a stranger to Romanticism, for most of the music we have known all our lives is romantic. Even the most unsophisticated listener, if he has experienced anything beyond popular music, usually prides himself on a humming knowledge of something late-romantic, perhaps a tune from Tchaikovsky's Romeo and Juliet, or an abridged version of parts of Rachmaninoff's Second Concerto. And what matter if this first contact with serious music is made through a popular adaptation fitted out with cloying words? Occasionally this painless introduction leads to an acquaintance with the rest of the piece, and who knows how much further?

It is almost a rule that romantic music unlocks the door to music's realm for those among the uninitiated who care to enter. Once inside, the pathways of Romanticism may lead via Beethoven to Classicism, via Liszt's transcriptions to Bach, or via Debussy to the whole kaleidoscope of twentieth-century music. Nor is this esthetic progression restricted to the non-musician. Many a young music student experiences early an overpowering infatuation with the sensuality of the nineteenth century, often through its most obvious or noisy examples, perhaps Liszt's Les Preludes or the 1812 Overture.

Moreover, before Romanticism can lead the listener from Beethoven to Mozart it often leads him to Schubert, or perhaps at the other end of the century from Tchaikovsky to Brahms. For within the romantic era itself, there is an immense span in style, quality, and intensity of personal expression—from the transitional works of Beethoven or the barely romantic Mendelssohn to the rich and highly spiced fare of Wagner and Richard Strauss. It is indeed possible, though not recommended, to spend an entire musical lifetime within the boundaries of this amazing century. Even granting its limitations, discrimination and taste can in fact develop within the romantic world itself. Unfortunately, in the vast output of the period many very good composers —Heller, Grieg, Gade—were eclipsed by the imposing figures that remain. And of course others were mercifully forgotten—the Chaminades, the Scharwenkas. No one, however, challenges the stature of those Romantics whom history has sifted out and whose works have become "classic." To the piano student they represent the main course of a balanced musical diet. Problems in a new society amid new social conventions and political philosophies forced the romantic composer to find adequate resources for what were then utterly new types of musical thought. This led to important innovations regarding sonorities, techniques of composition, forms and harmonies.

New Sonorities

Very important to the development of Romanticism was the possibility for new sounds The piano of the 1840's, a vastly different mechanism from Mozart's instrument, almost demanded the exploration of its tonal possibilities. These new piano sounds were paralleled by those of the evolving modern symphony orchestra, another perfect vehicle for romantic thought. Romanticism might have flickered out without these two media so admirably suited to its needs.

The romantic composers needed no prompting to take advantage of these new worlds of sound. Consider the utter consternation that must have greeted Schumann's thundering chords in the *Carnaval* or the *Symphonic Etudes!* Who had ever imagined a piano so triumphant? And Chopin's magic—the incredible colors he evoked with intricate bass figurations or decorative filigrees! Liszt learned much from him and carried matters even further. Composers for the piano, with the exception of the French Impressionists, have, in fact, found very little new in tonal possibilities since they were so thoroughly explored by this great trio.

New Techniques Of Composition

New techniques in composition developed simultaneously with the evolution of new instrumental resources, advances which were made at the cost of immense pioneering effort. However, in keeping with the romantic imagination, popular legend has made a cliché of the neurotic, self-focused romantic composer, in the throes of either anguish or exaltation, scribbling in a frenzy of midnight inspiration from which would emerge a masterwork. Unfortunately this picture has only the slightest relation to the truth. The romantic era was one of tremendous craftsmanship. It did not produce fugues of the intellectual and emotional depth of Bach's, but it did give us the fugues of Beethoven's late sonatas, in which emotional fervor combines with an individual craftsmanship quite different from Bach's, but perhaps not inferior.

Or take the Chopin myths, for example his allegedly composing the "Raindrop Prelude" in an agony of anxiety while George Sand was prevented by a torrential rain-storm in the mountains around Valdemosa, from returning to the monastery cell they shared. Chopin, the most meticulous craftsman of the romantic era, the perfectionist who could not leave off revision of a work until the moment he sent it to the publisher, seems ludicrously out of place in these popular fantasies. Incidentally the "cell" was a four-room apartment with a private garden and a twenty mile view.

Schumann, too, suffers from a popularized distortion, Schumann the "amateur," the self-taught composer, the renegade law student, half musician, half writer. Some of these are fact. He was a true original, the most original of all the Romanticists. But, although his early training was unorthodox and in some areas a bit sketchy, he was certainly not one to consider the discipline of conventional studies irrelevant. With what intensity did he study counterpoint, and how he strove for a polish like Mendelssohn's! Fortunately his own virtues far outshone the polish he never achieved.

The thing we find difficult to imagine is the utter newness of the problem the Romantics posed for themselves. To express musically, for the first time in history, the most intimate nuances of personal feeling required imagination and a capacity for experimentation on a scale never needed before. When one considers that their only inherited resources were the forms and sounds of classicism, their achievement seems truly miraculous. It is impossible for us to analyze the evolution of their creative processes; we can only concede, on the basis of the splendid evidence they have left us, that the evolution occurred.

New Forms

A persistent and erroneous notion pictures the Romantics as uninterested in form. Actually one of the first problems they had to solve was that of form. The question must have presented itself to each of them: can new and different musical ideas be made to fit the older forms, or, more precisely, can the older forms serve as vehicles for new ideas? A second question followed: If the old forms will not serve, what new forms can be found or invented?

Each composer answered these questions differently. Fortunately some found the sonata form still usable as a vehicle for the emotional content of romantic music. Schubert and Mendelssohn managed quite well without modifying it, probably because of a large residue of classical feeling in their makeup. So did Brahms much later. Even Chopin changed the sonata only slightly.

Beethoven, on the contrary, after the early years when he wrote sonatas as orthodox as anyone's, merely longer, found the form inadequate to his later more romantic concepts. Never one to bend his ideas to fit any preconceived mold, he twisted the sonata into strange new shapes appropriate to expression that becomes at times as personal as Brahms'.

Schumann shunned the classical forms in his piano music except occasionally. When he did write his first sonata (Op. 11) he produced one of the earliest examples of a cyclical form by using materials from the first movement as a basis for the slow movement.

More significant were the forms that were invented during the period. Chopin, in the *Ballades* and the *Fantasy,* created tightly-knit formal structures that definitely were not sonatas, not rondos, not anything known before, yet were suitable for extended works, as suitable in fact as the sonata. Schumann did the same in his *Fantasy;* in other compositions, *Kreisleriana,* for example, he found ways of creating large works by joining smaller units, varying in size and number from one composition to the next. Liszt sometimes paraphrased poetry, the sonnets of Petrarch, and the "Consolations" of Saint-Beuve.

Formally conventional but new in character were the Nocturnes, Impromptus, Intermezzi, and other smaller types which proliferated in this period, and which were ideal for romantic thought in smaller dimension. Indeed, most characteristic of all may have been the miniatures, the tiny, perfectly formed gems like Chopin's *Preludes,* Schumann's *Fantasy Pieces,* or Mendelssohn's *Songs Without Words.* Here were gestures which seemed to say that, in spite of other works on a massive scale that were produced in the same era, size in itself does not count, that the solitary diamond is intrinsically as beautiful as the imperial crown, ornate with rubies and emeralds; a genuinely romantic idea.

Harmonic Innovations

Harmonic vocabulary adjusted itself rapidly to the need for personal expression. Schubert's shifting modulations and waverings between major and minor, Liszt's daring chromaticisms, Schumann's chains of suspensions, Chopin's complete unorthodoxy, all were suited to the needs of romantic music. Other composers found other very personal solutions, such as Brahms' bitter-sweet semi-dissonances. In fact, the harmonic vocabulary of romanticism proved so versatile that only sheer frustration eventually drove twentieth century composers to the exploration of new paths of sound and meaning.

Looking back, none of the technical or creative factors we have been considering seem to fit the supposed trance-like inspiration of the romantic composers of popular legend. They were, on the contrary, hard-working artists, inspired and emotionally driven as well, but with creative minds as dedicated as Bach's. Herein lies the real reason why their imagination and inspiration still have wonderful things to say to us today.

Performing Romantic Music

Although we were all brought up on romantic music, perhaps a few comments on its performance would not be out of place. The whole gamut of modern piano technique developed during this period, and in fact has been enlarged very little since. In the baroque and classical periods the pianist could consider his technique as being a concern of his fingers only. Haydn's or Mozart's occasional use of octaves was exceptional enough not to impress or frighten the performer with a consciousness of their lack in his equipment.

With Beethoven this digital self-sufficiency was shattered. In addition to his enormous demands on the fingers, chords became bothersome as they assumed more significance. Octaves were no longer a rarity, and broken octaves, a Beethoven obsession, tested the endurance of unaccustomed wrists. The important role of wrists and arms, in fact, was discovered at this point. In many a work after Beethoven they even crowded the fingers from first place as a technical problem.

The immense variety of virtuoso techniques that developed, Liszt's pyrotechnics, Chopin's filigrees, Schumann's chordal audacities, Brahms' athletic prowess, all helped develop generations of pianistic giants. Curiously enough, this legitimate virtuosity was to serve in the education of a naive public. For in this age when all concert-goers craved display, the presence of such spectacular elements in the great music of the romantics began to lure the public from the showy nonsense then offered by Herz, Hünten, Döhler and their confrères.

With these virtuoso techniques we are all to some degree familiar, just as we are with the huge literature of instructive material that began to appear during the period —études, exercises, "schools of piano playing"—all intended to facilitate the mastery of romanticism's rhetoric. And we are still trying to master it.

Pedalling became a fine art with romantic music. Though clarity was still a virtue, it lost its pre-eminence as the one indispensable quality. Sometimes it was deliberately sacrificed in order to achieve the tonal effects, incredible in their day, sought by Chopin or Liszt. Pedal technique thus became more demanding as the ear became more fastidious.

Melody playing, above all, is the trade-mark of the romantic pianist, for it is usually the most important single factor in the music he plays. One should mention the balancing of the melody line against the other parts, in most romantic music the source of beauty of tone. Here we find intensified the familiar hierarchy of sound in which the melody line must predominate, closely followed in importance by the bass line, both supported and colored by discreetly treated inner figurations and chords. Even Chopin's late use of polyphony does not usually disturb this fundamental one-two-three balance.

The one most dangerous element in romantic performance is that risky condiment, rubato. A give and take in the rhythmic flow is the very essence of good romantic playing; without it the performance sounds dull and meaningless, but with too much, a performance can sound absurd, if not downright sickening. One cannot blame today's talented high-school girl, who, turning to the piano instead of to Rock as an outlet for romantic fantasy, exploits a Chopin Nocturne or wrings the ultimate tear from one of Rachmaninoff's sighing melodies. But with advancing taste and judgment one realizes that rubato is much like garlic in cooking. Used subtly, garlic can be one of the crowning touches of the *haute cuisine.* Used blatantly, it can spoil otherwise good cookery. Rubato is the spice of romantic performance.

This Volume

Included, of course, are representative works, among them some of the best known, from all the greatest Romanticists. In addition one will find pieces by excellent composers who were overshadowed by the giants. Grieg, for example, was a worthy, dedicated, and skillful composer. Nationalism, a leading musical trait in the nine-teenth century, seems to have gotten the better of him, with the result that he became repetitious and missed greatness by a very thin margin. Much of his music especially in the smaller forms, is utterly delightful.

Heller is another whose early promise, acclaimed by Schumann, fell somewhat short of unquestioned greatness. He has, however, left us many first-rate piano pieces which deserve far more attention than is generally accorded to them. Others, Tchaikovsky, Hugo Wolf, Glinka, who left relatively little piano music are presented in samples which reflect qualities usually demonstrated in their works for other media. Finally, certain great composers like Rachmaninoff, Franck, or Fauré have written extensively for piano but usually on more difficult levels; we have chosen works which should give an acquaintance with their styles and an incentive to playing their more advanced pieces later.

Above all, romantic music is to be enjoyed. The notion that one should somehow be analyzing music while he listens to it is particularly out of place here. In our time we are experiencing a healthy decline in suspicion of emotion, and a willingness to let ourselves be moved by romantic music as were the young rebels of 1830. It is our hope that this volume may both aid in this evolution and make its progress more enjoyable.

After all, in the entire history of music only the composers of the nineteenth century have wished and have been able to transform into sound the fears, loves, joys, and despairs we all experience and usually manage to suppress or conceal. The catharsis offered by Schubert, Brahms, or Chopin is a gift of incalculable value. Let the poets try, as they always have, to do the same thing; the musician knows that music does it much better.

Two "Valses Sentimentales"

Moderato

Franz Schubert

1.

2.

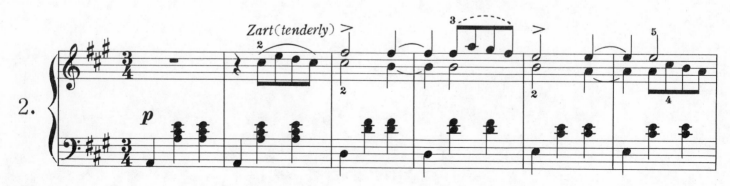

Six Ländler

from Op. 33 and Op. 67

Franz Schubert

1.

2.

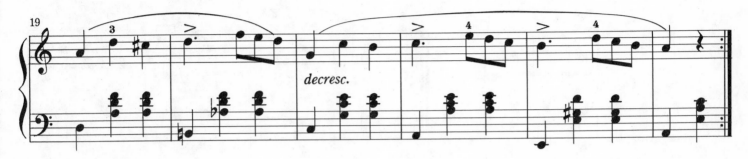

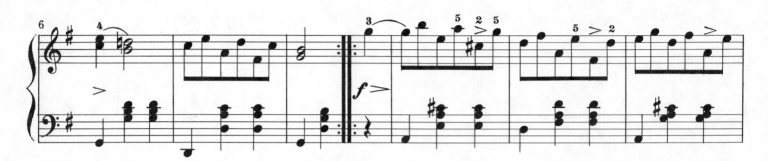

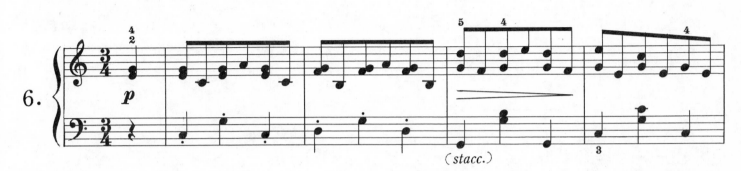

6.

23

Allegretto

Franz Schubert

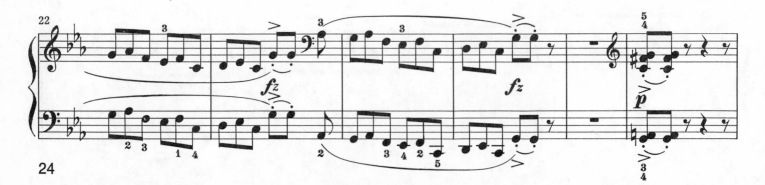

24

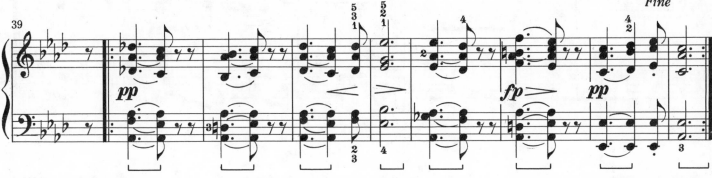

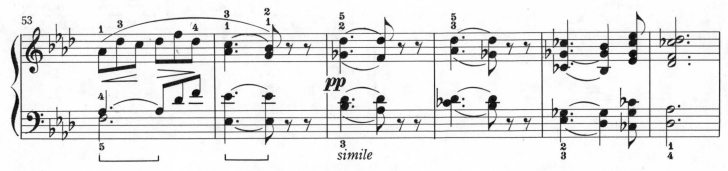

D.C. senza repetizione

Moment Musical

Op. 94, No. 3

Franz Schubert

Allegro moderato

(staccato sempre)

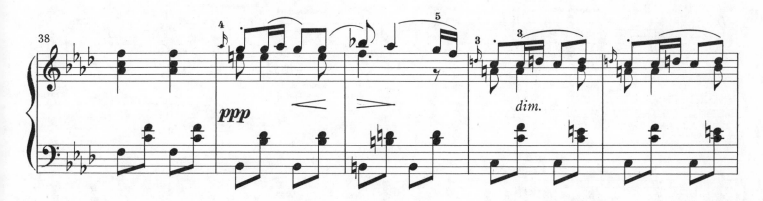

Moment Musical

Op. 94, No. 2

Franz Schubert

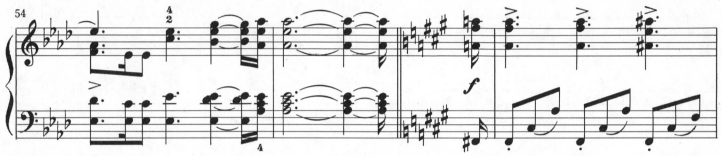

(simile)

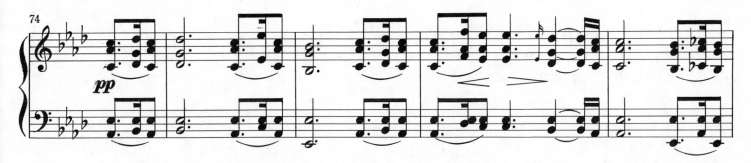

Five Ecossaises

Franz Schubert

1.

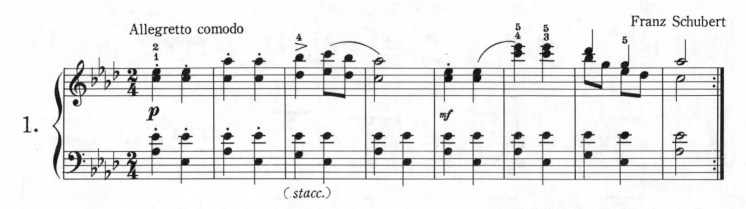

2.

No. 1 D.C.

3.

32

Allegretto comodo

4.

(stacc.)

No. 3 D.C.

Allegretto con moto

5.

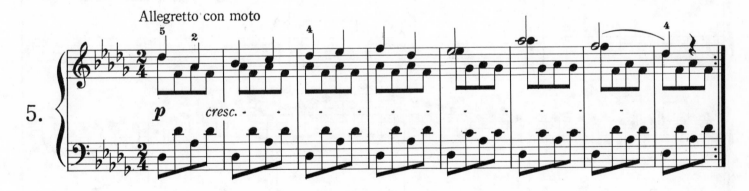

Impromptu

Op. 90, No. 2

Franz Schubert

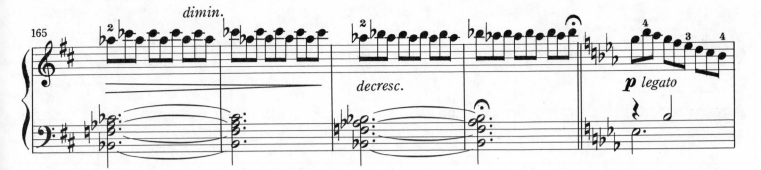

Coda

Melody

Op. 68, No. 1

Robert Schumann

First Loss
Op. 68, No. 16

Nicht schnell (Not fast) ♩ = 96

Robert Schumann

44

The Reapers' Song

Op. 68, No. 18

Robert Schumann

Nicht sehr schnell (Not very fast) ♩ =120

Italian Sailors' Song
Op. 68, No. 36

Langsam (Slowly)　　　Schnell (Fast)　　　　Robert Schumann

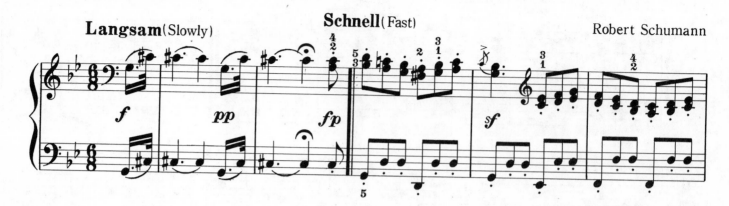

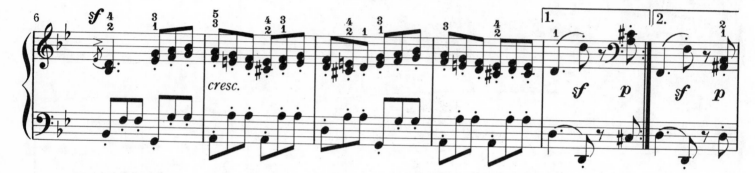

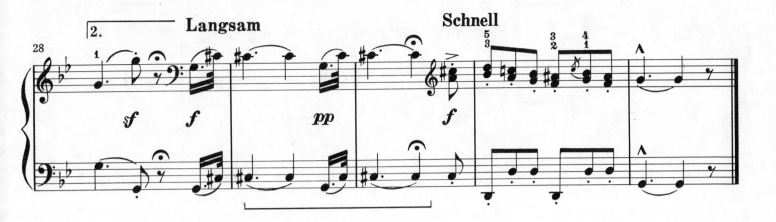

Child Falling Asleep

Op. 15, No. 12

Robert Schumann

Important Event

Op. 15, No. 6

Robert Schumann

At The Inn

Herberge, Op. 82, No. 6

Robert Schumann

Mässig (Moderately) ♩ = 130

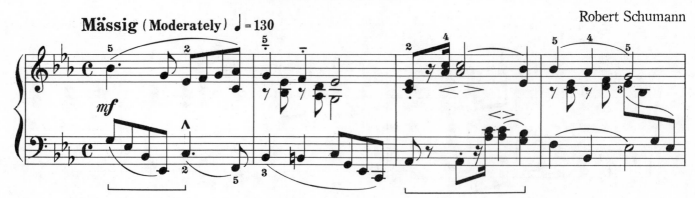

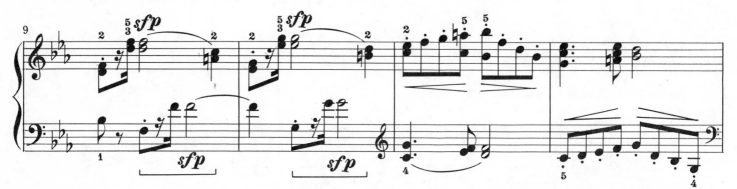

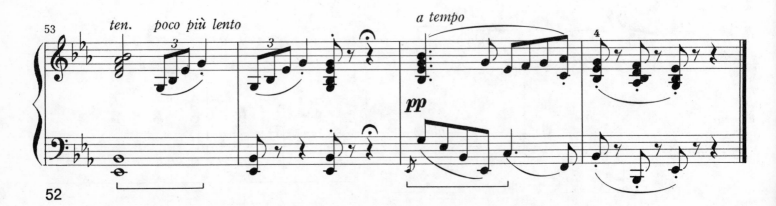

The Prophet Bird

Vogel als Prophet, Op. 82, No. 7

Langsam, sehr zart (Slow, very tender) ♩ = 63

Robert Schumann

Etwas langsamer (Somewhat slower)

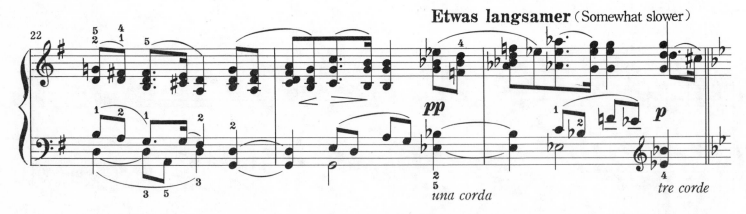

una corda

tre corde

Im Tempo

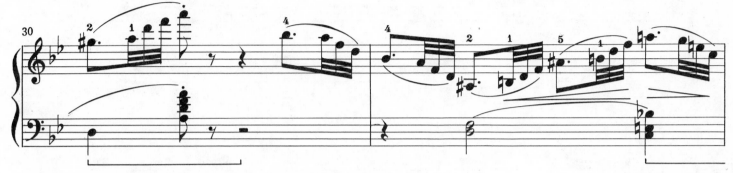

Phantasy Dance

Phantasietanz, Op. 124, No.5

Sehr rasch (**Very swift**) ♩ = 124

Robert Schumann

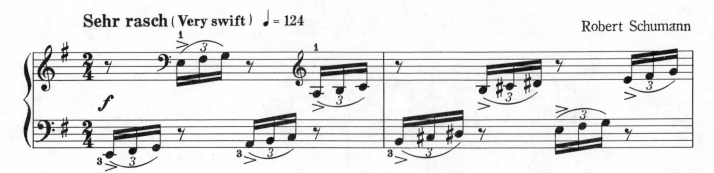

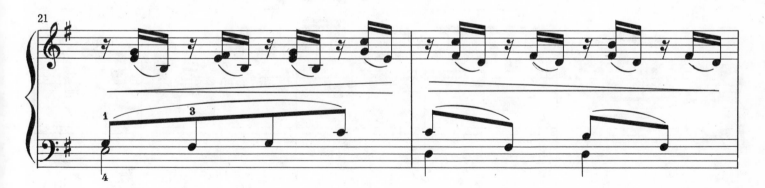

Two "Davidsbündler" Dances

Op. 6, Nos. 11, 12

Robert Schumann

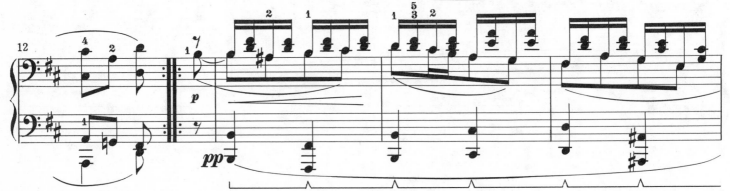

ad libitum Da Capo

Mit Humor ♩ = 104

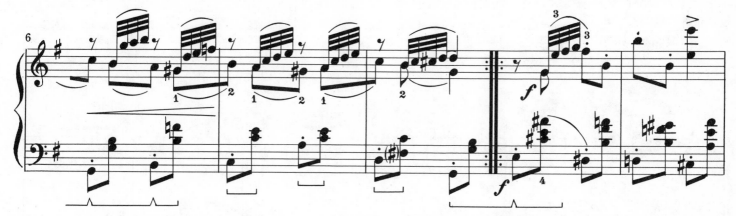

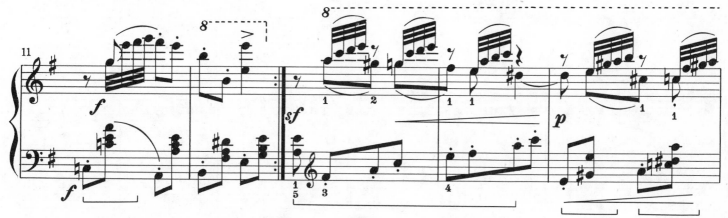

F

Novellette

Op. 99, No. 9

Robert Schumann

Lebhaft (Lively)

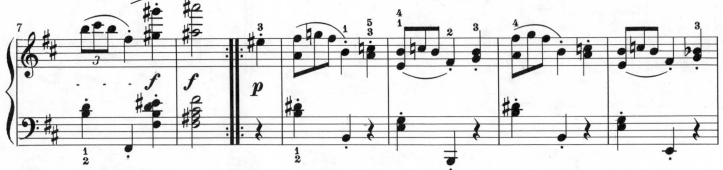

60

Romanze

Op. 28, No. 2

Robert Schumann

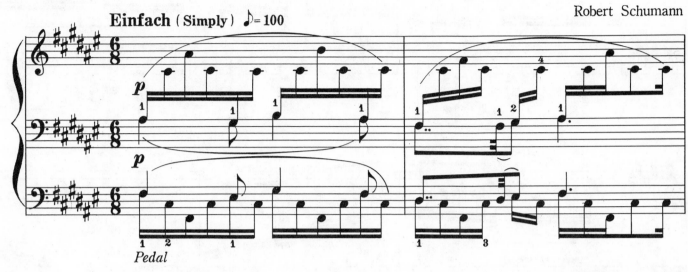

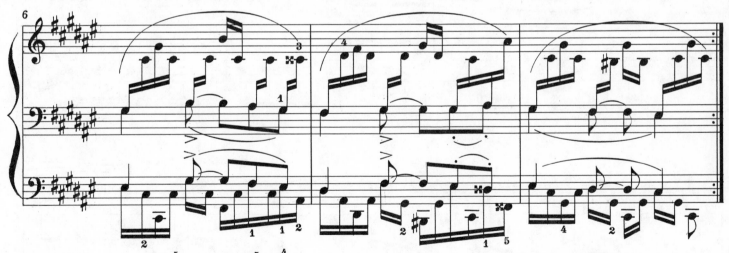

Intermezzo
Op. 26, No. 4

Robert Schumann

Mit größter Energie ♩ = 104

Ped. simile

Ped. simile

Soaring

Aufschwung, Op. 12, No. 2

Robert Schumann

Sehr rasch (Very fast)

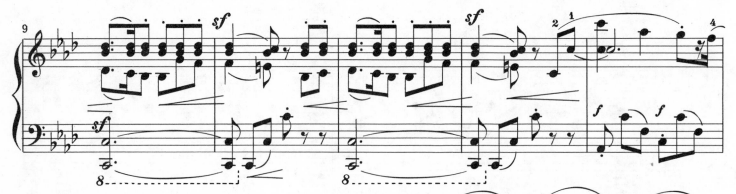

Silent Night

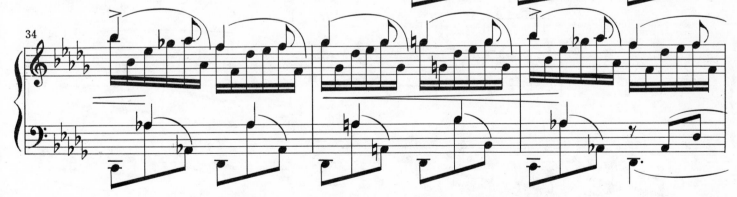

73

74

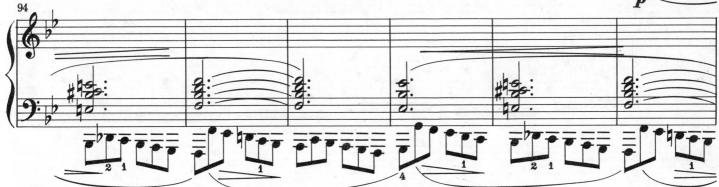

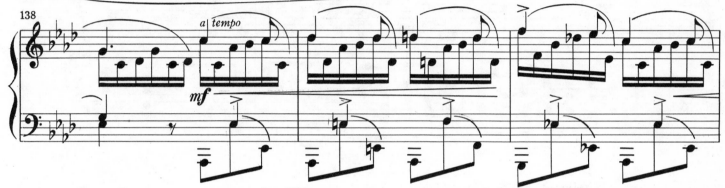

Song Without Words

Op. 53, No. 4

Felix Mendelssohn - Bartholdy

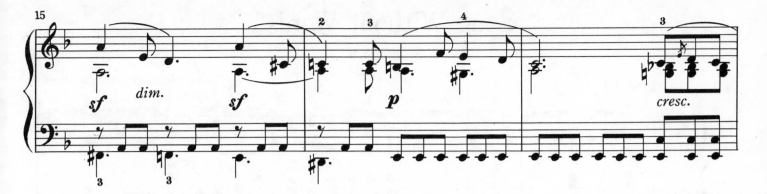

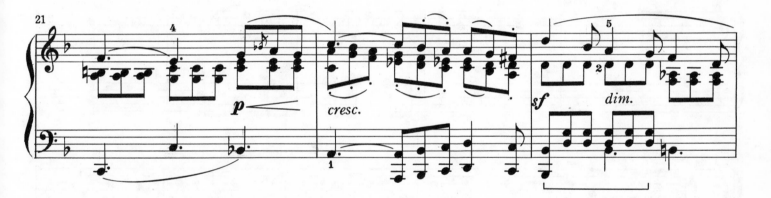

Song Without Words

Op. 102, No. 3

Felix Mendelssohn-Bartholdy

Presto

Venetian Boat Song

Op. 19, No. 6

Felix Mendelssohn-Bartholdy

Andante sostenuto

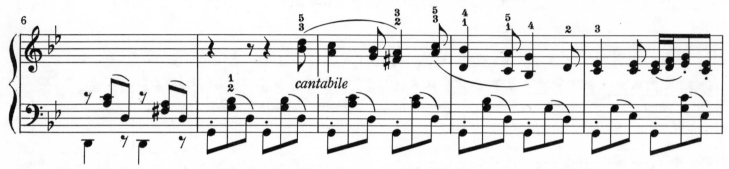

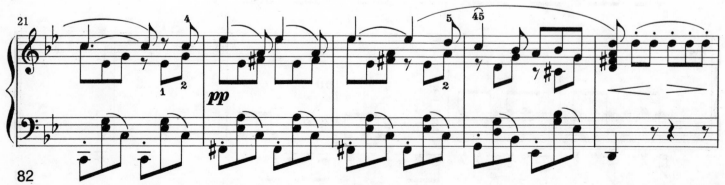

83

Scherzo

Op. 16, No. 2

Felix Mendelssohn-Bartholdy

Presto

84

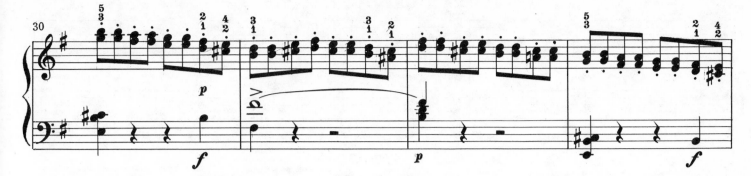

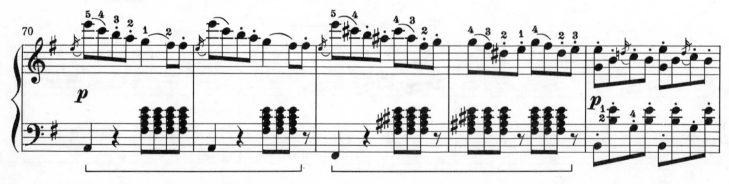

Mazurka
Op.7, No. 2

Frédéric Chopin

Vivo, ma non troppo ♩ = 160

(Ped. simile)

Mazurka

Op. 17, No. 1

Frédéric Chopin

Vivo e risoluto ♩ = 160

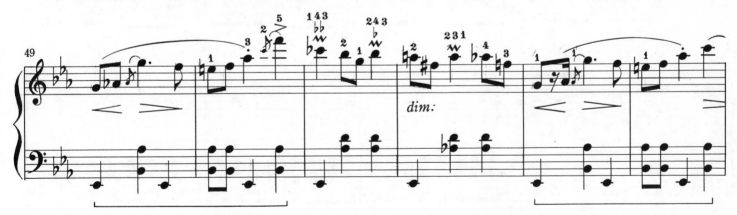

D.C. al Fine

Prelude
Op.28, No.4

Frédéric Chopin

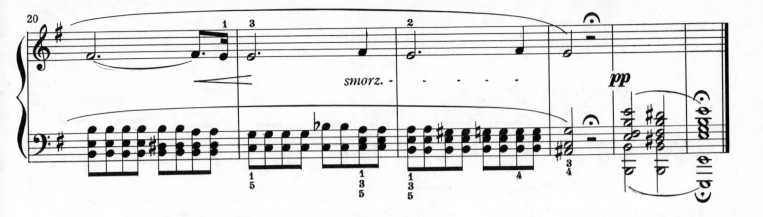

Prelude

Op. 28, No. 7

Frédéric Chopin

Andantino

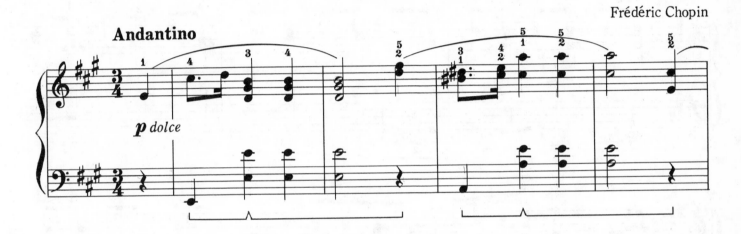

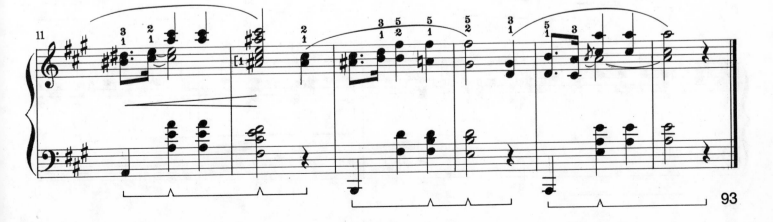

Prélude

Op. 28, No. 6

Frédéric Chopin

Assai lento

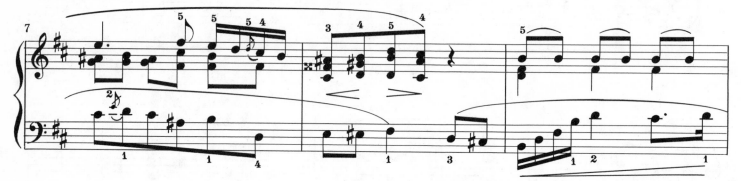

Prelude

Op. 28, No. 20

Frédéric Chopin

Prelude
Op. 28, No. 15

Frédéric Chopin

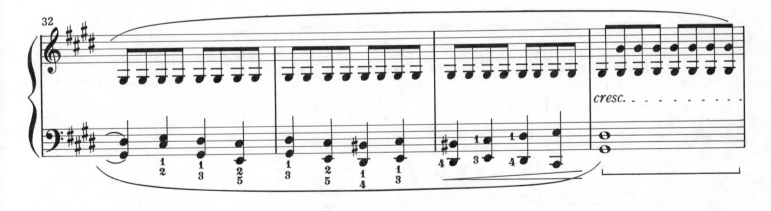

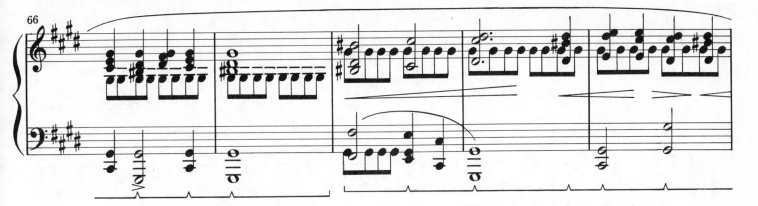

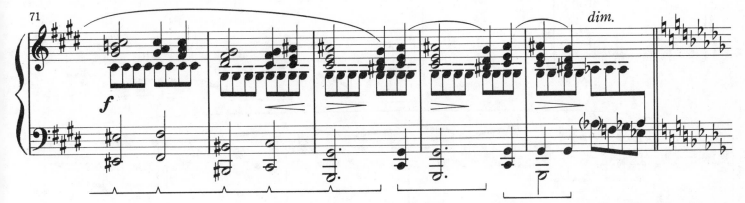

Prelude

Op. 28, No.11

Frédéric Chopin

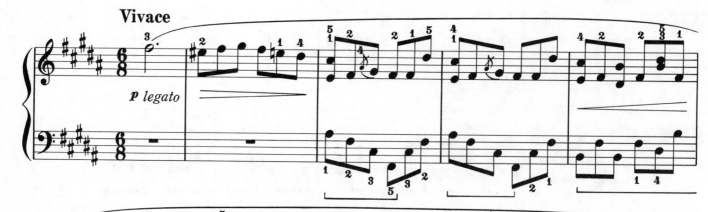

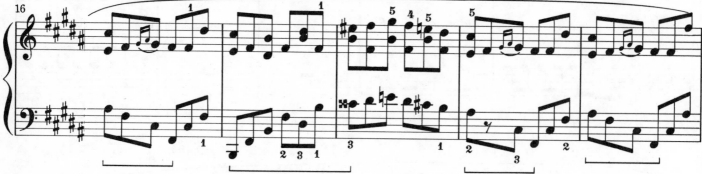

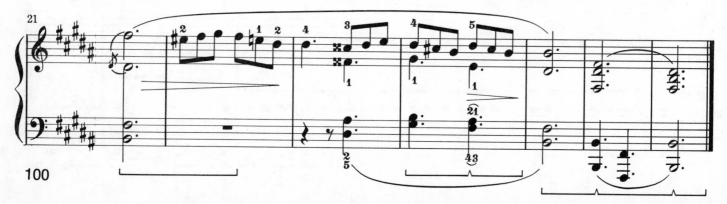

Nocturne

Op. 55, No. 1

Frédéric Chopin

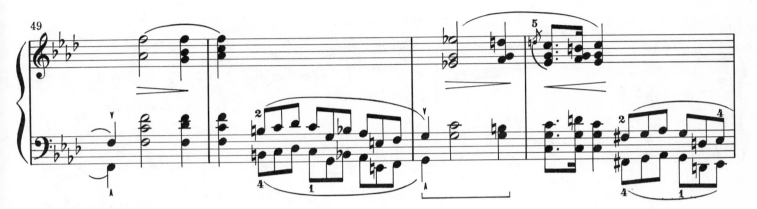

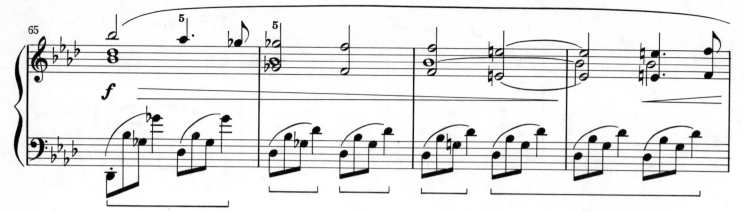

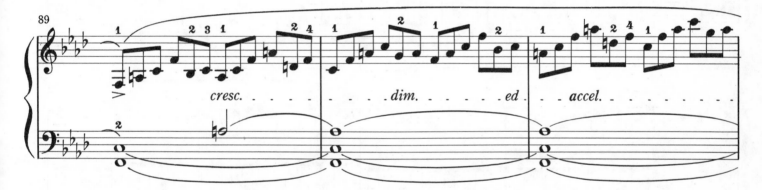

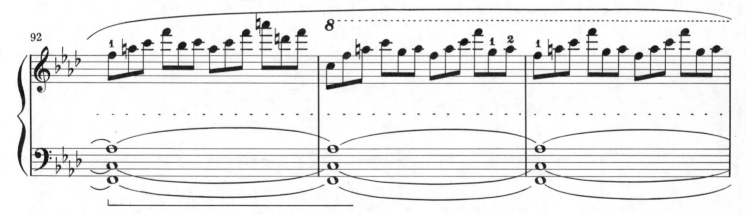

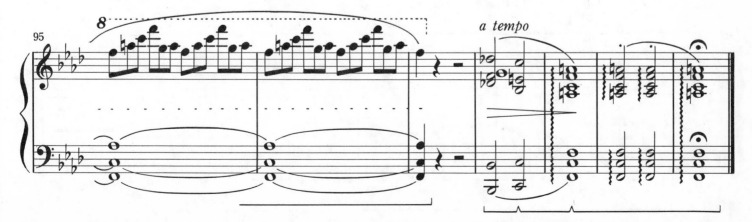

Nocturne

Op. 27, No. 1

Frédéric Chopin

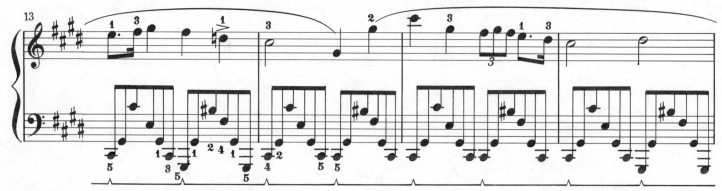

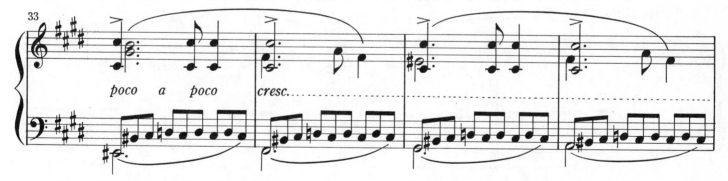

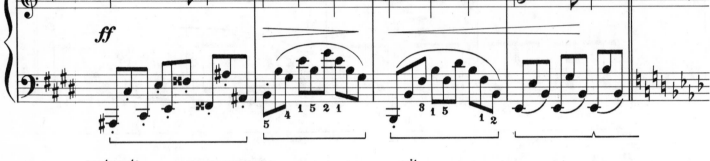

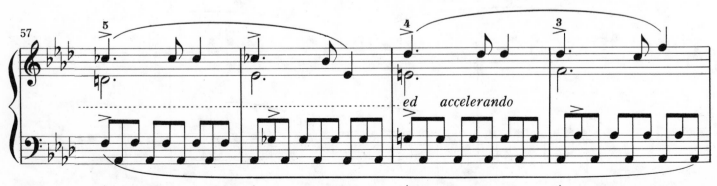

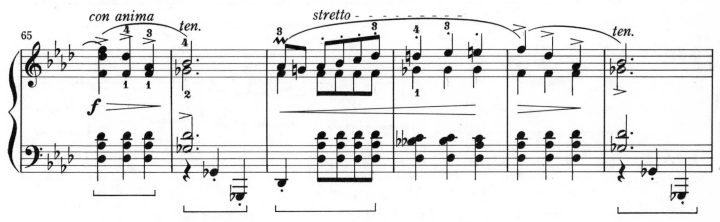

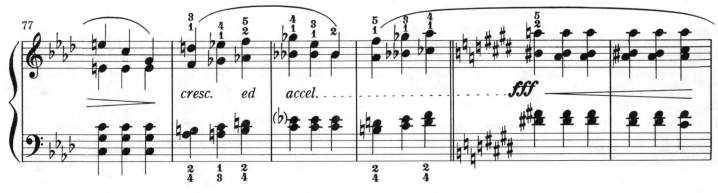

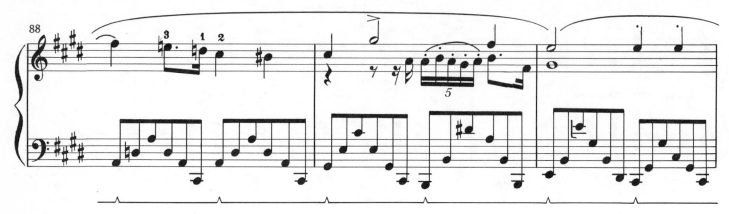

Valse

(Opus Postumum)

Frédéric Chopin

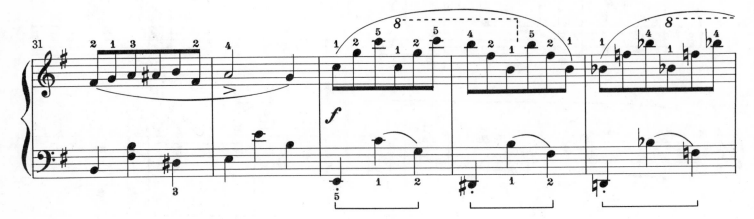

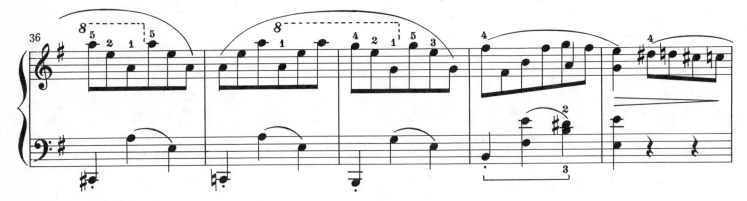

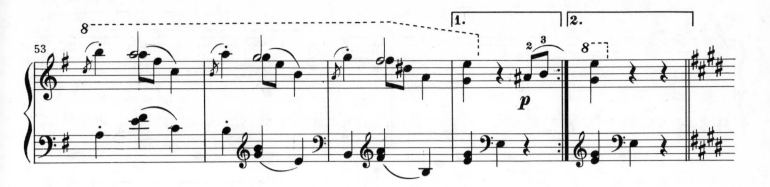

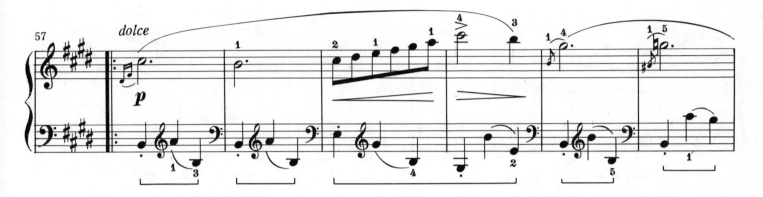

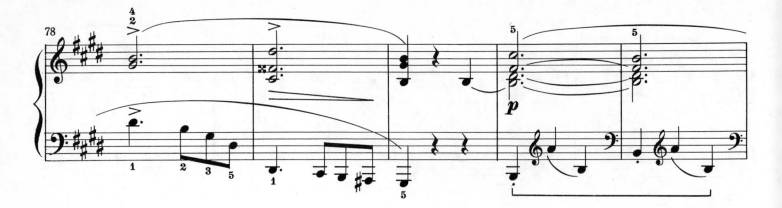

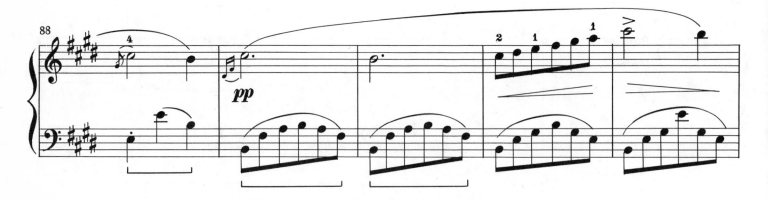

Ped. come prima

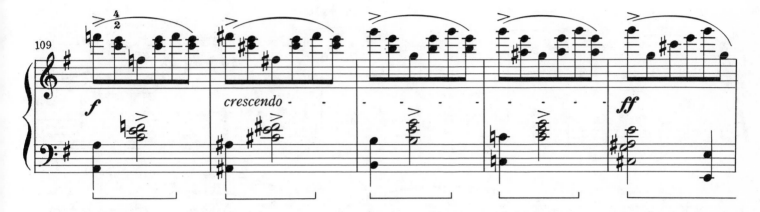

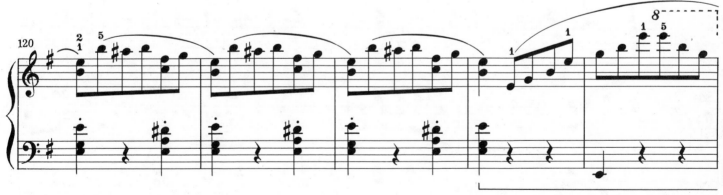

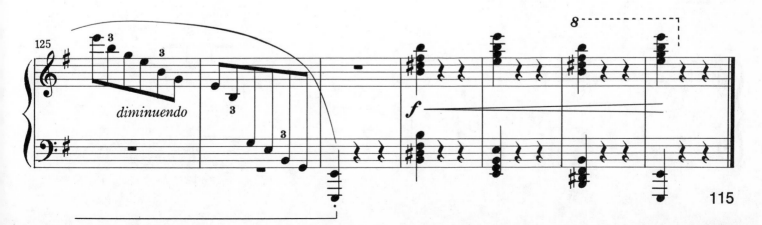

Valse

Op. 69, No. 1

Frédéric Chopin

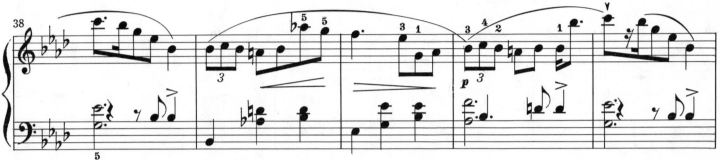

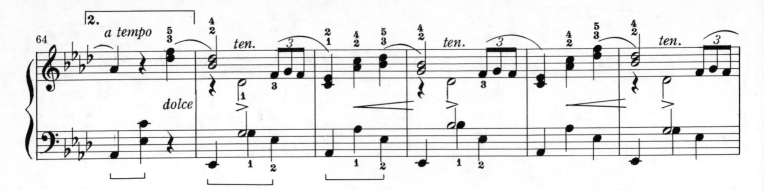

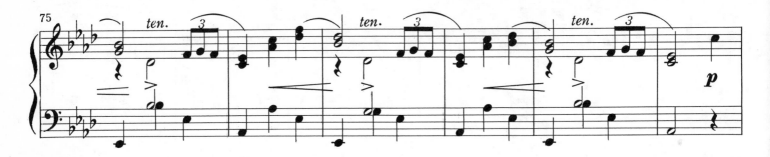

118

Etude

Op. 10, No. 3

Frédéric Chopin

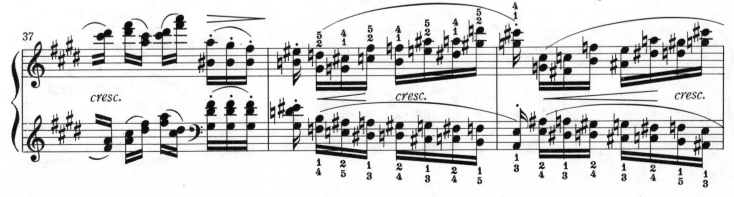

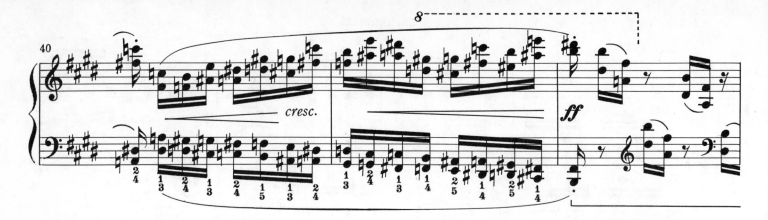

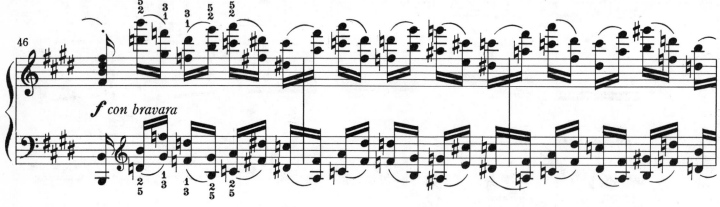

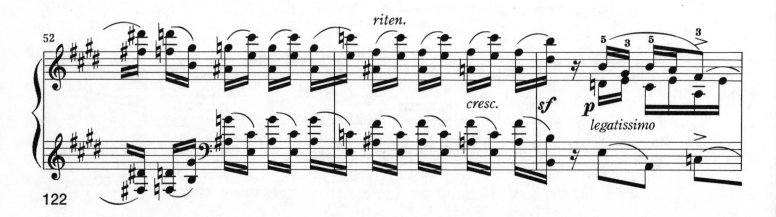

Etude

Op. 25, No. 2

Frédéric Chopin

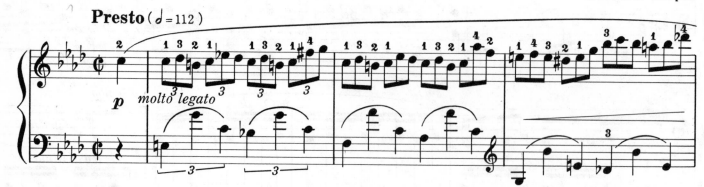

poco. . . . . . . a. . . . . . poco. . . . . cresc.

cresc. . . . .

f

p

poco riten.

smorz. . . . .

Polonaise
Op.26, No.1

Frédéric Chopin

Allegro appassionato

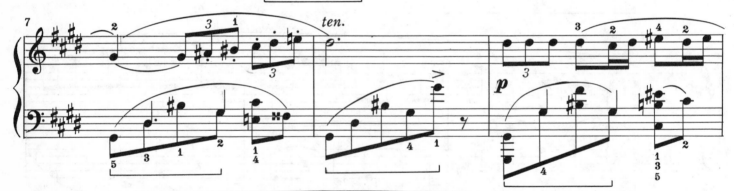

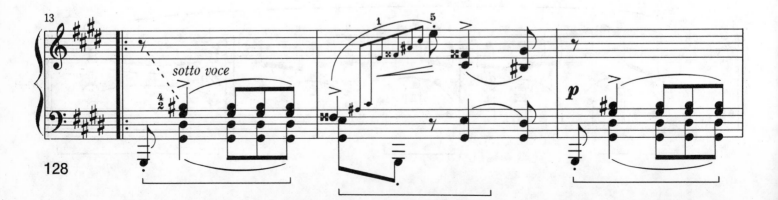

Fine

ben legato

Da Capo al Fine

Children's Polka

Intermezzo

Andantino con moto

Mikhail Ivanovich Glinka

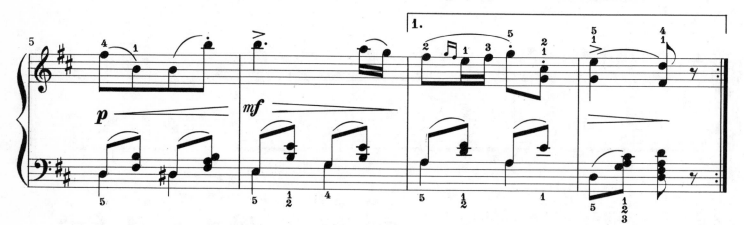

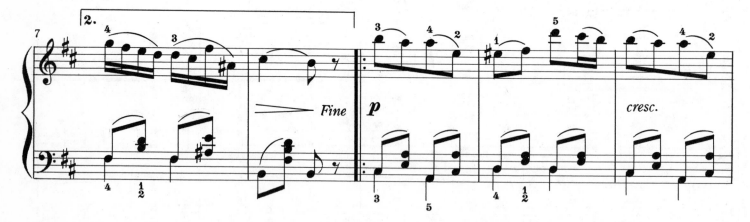

D.C. al Fine

Farewell Waltz

Mikhail Ivanovich Glinka

En Rêve

Nocturne

Franz Liszt

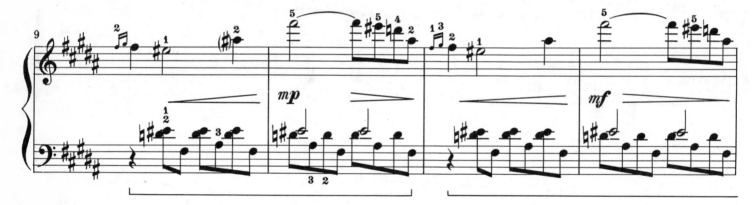

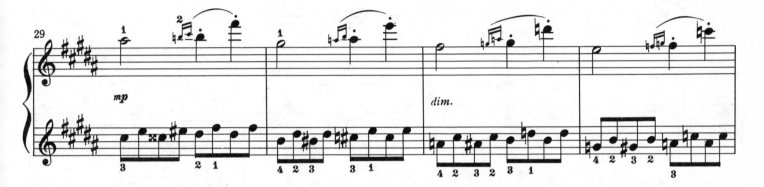

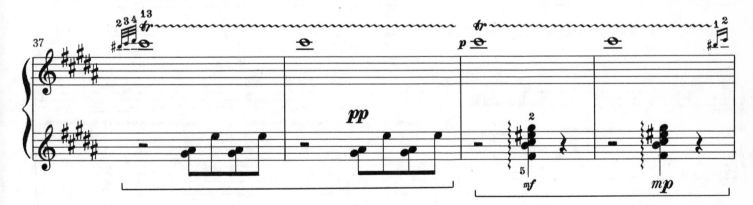

Consolation No. 3

Franz Liszt

Lento placido

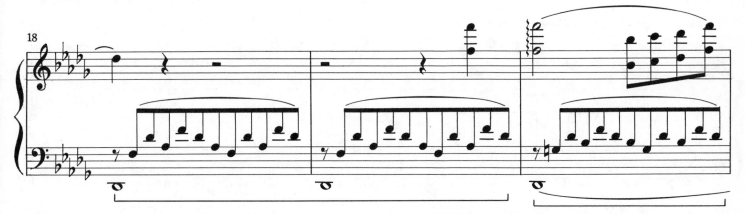

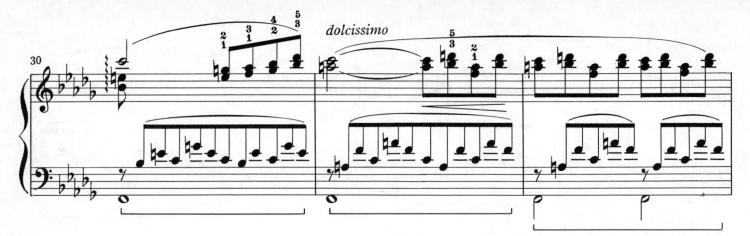

*These notes are additions by Emil von Sauer

Valse Oubliée

No. 1

Franz Liszt

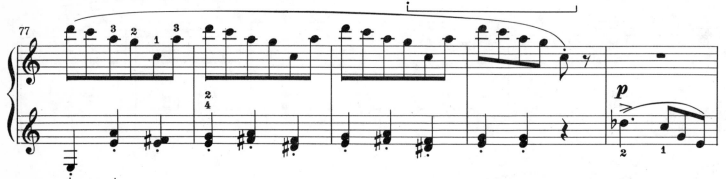

senza Ped.

p

p amoroso

⁵*legato*
sempre con Ped.

146

Elegie

Op. 19, No. 1

Niels Vilhelm Gade

Allegretto quasi andantino

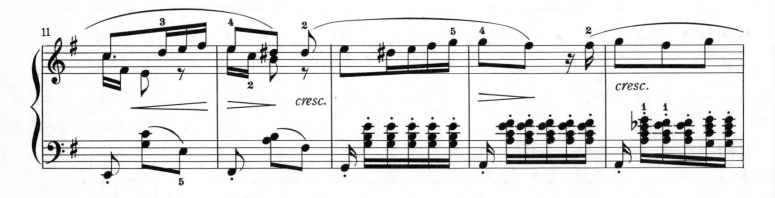

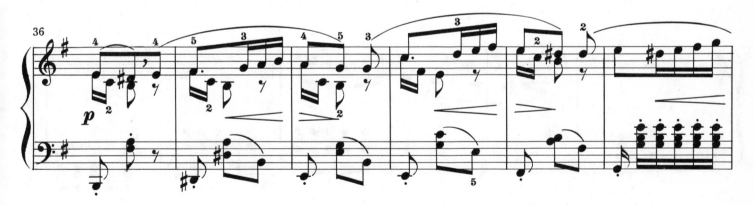

Prelude
Op. 119, No. 29

Stephen Heller

Andantino, quasi allegretto

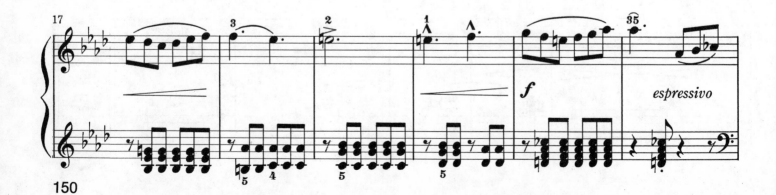

At Evening

Op. 138, No. 14

Stephen Heller

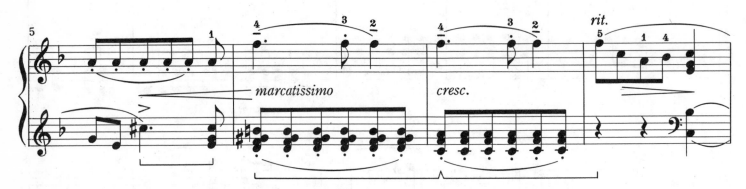

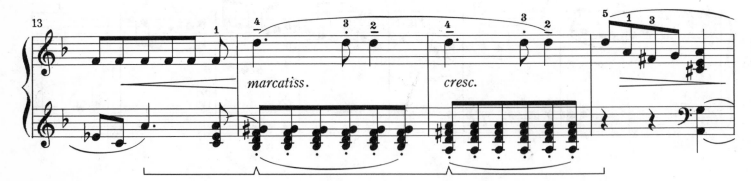

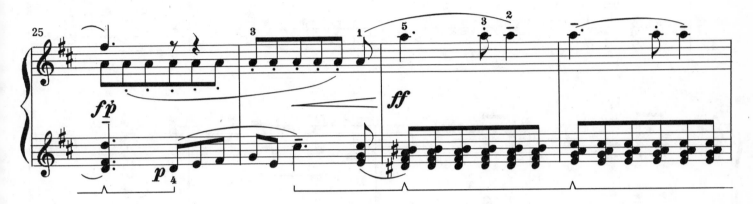

Scherzetto

Op.125, No.5

Stephen Heller

Un poco vivo (♩ = 108)

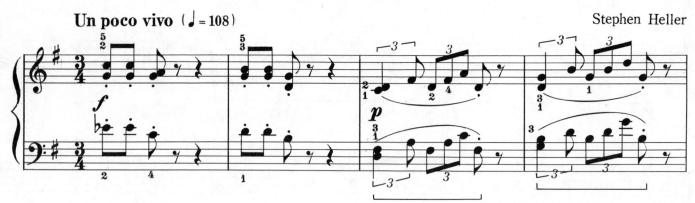

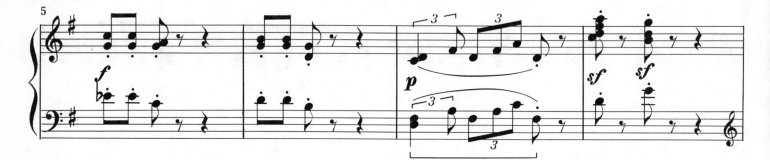

In The Village

Modeste Petrovich Moussorgsky

Larghetto; Quasi Fantasia

Grandioso; Meno mosso

marcato il canto

Allegretto scherzoso, non troppo allegro

cresc. e accel. *poco ritard.*

A tempo, non agitato (Alla zingara)

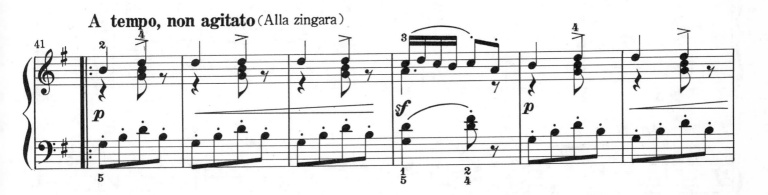

poco riten. *delicatissimo*

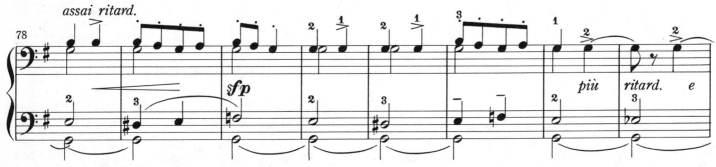

Tempo I Allegretto scherzoso

Poco a poco più vivo al fine; Capriccioso

Song of the Lark

Op. 39, No. 22

Peter Ilyich Tchaikovsky

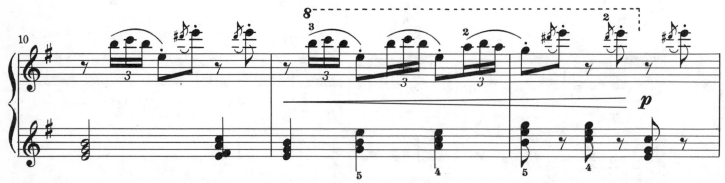

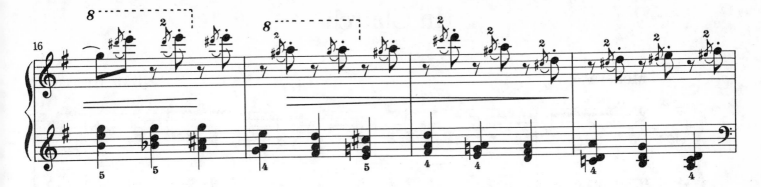

In Church
Op. 39, No. 24

Peter Ilyich Tchaikovsky

Moderato

Valse-Scherzo

No. 2, Op. 59

Peter I. Tchaikovsky

Allegro, in tempo di Valse

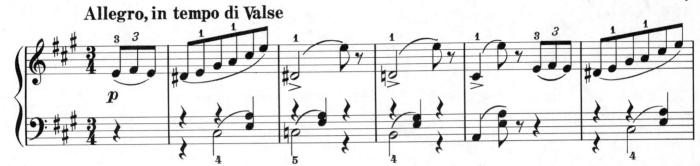

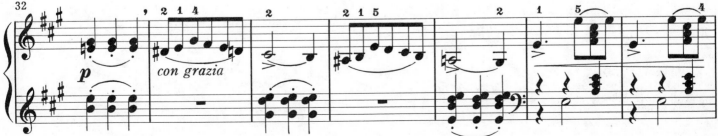

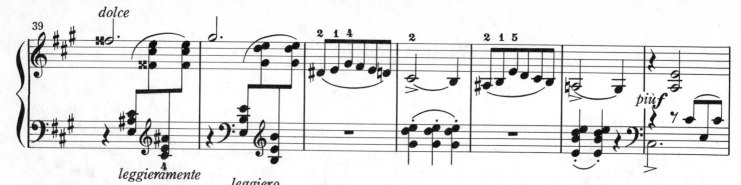

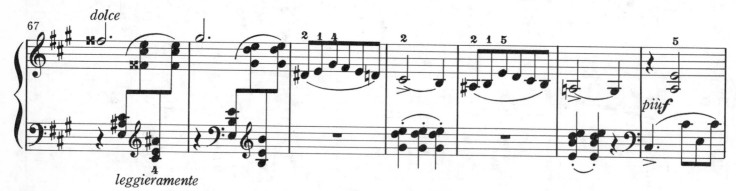

Chanson Triste

Op. 40, No. 2

Allegro non troppo

la melodia con molto espressione

Peter Ilyich Tchaikovsky

Grandmother's Songs

Op. 27, Nos. 10 and 8

1.

Andantino con tenerezza

Robert Volkmann

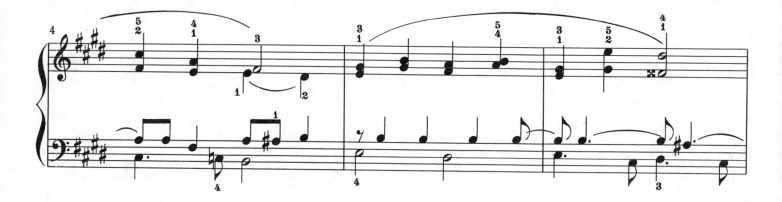

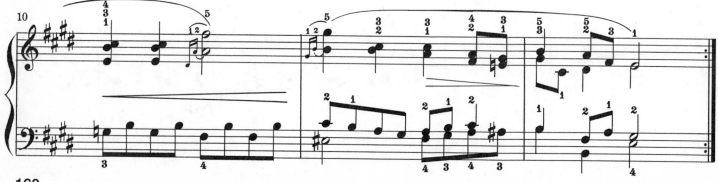

2.

Moderato; serioso

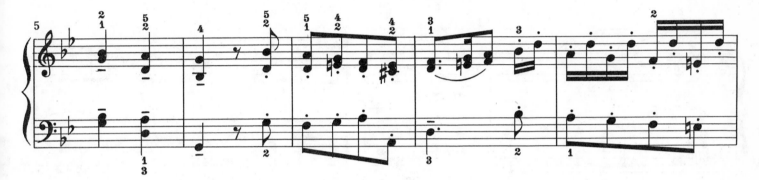

Idyl

Op. 4, No. 2

Bedrich Smetana

Moderato ma non troppo

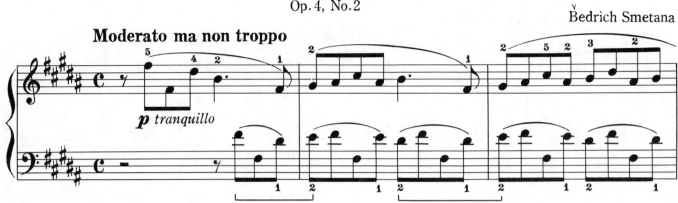

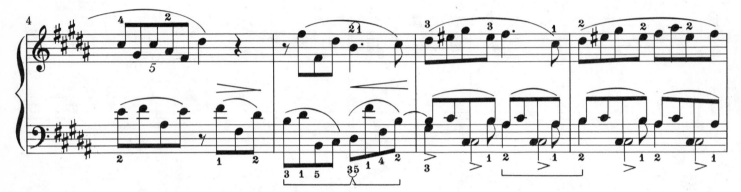

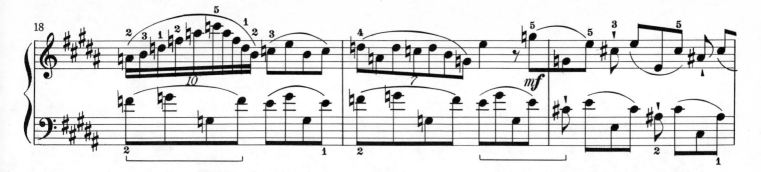

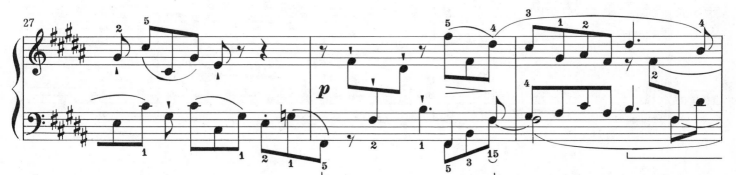

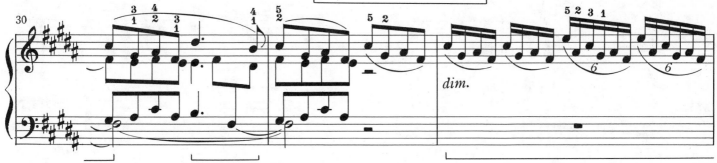

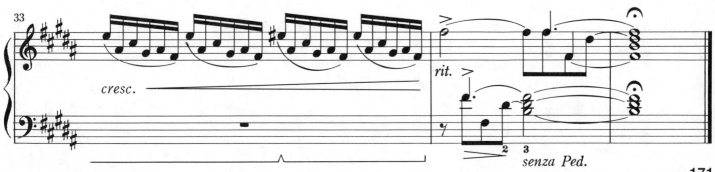

Polka

Op. 53

Antonin Dvořák

Poco allegro

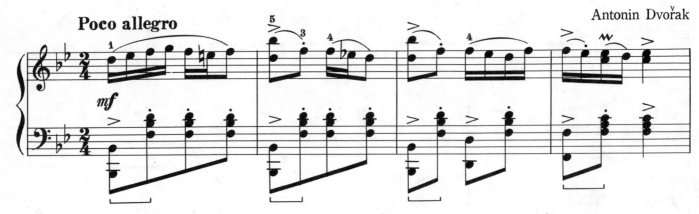

Fine

Trio

Silhouette

Op. 8, No. 2

Antonin Dvořák

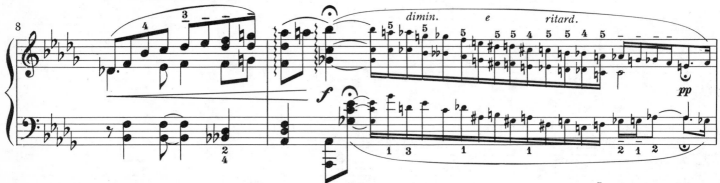

174

Barcarolle

Op. 65, No. 6

Assez lentement (Quite slowly)

Charles-Valentin Alkan

Four Waltzes

Op. 39, Nos. 1, 2, 3 and 15

1

Johannes Brahms

Tempo giusto

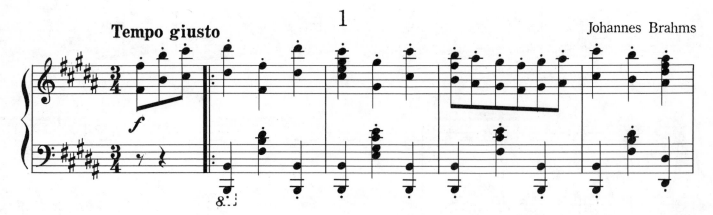

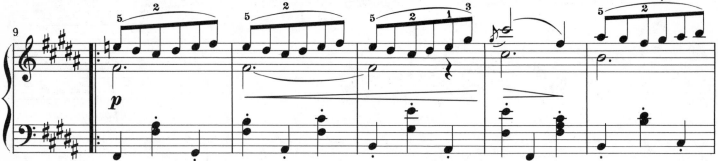

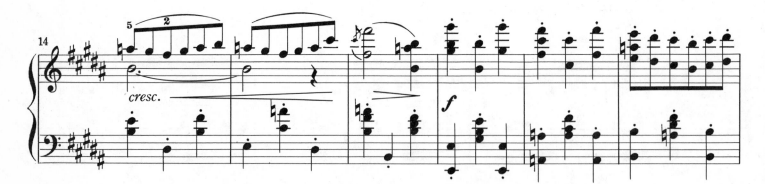

2

3

4

Hungarian Dance No. 7

Allegretto vivace

Johannes Brahms

Rhapsody

Op.79, No.2

Johannes Brahms

Molto passionato, ma non troppo allegro

186

188

Intermezzo

Op. 117, No. 1

Johannes Brahms

Andante moderato

Più adagio

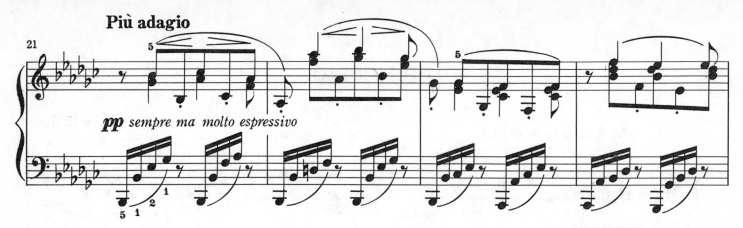

Un poco più andante

Intermezzo

Op. 119, No. 3

Johannes Brahms

Grazioso e giocoso

molto **p** *e leggiero*

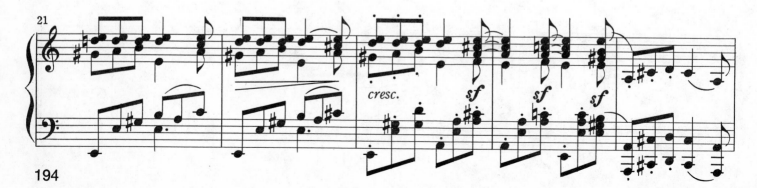

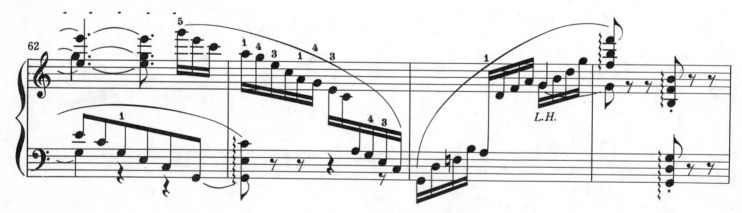

Little Prelude

(C minor)

César Franck

Poco lento

Little Prelude

(E-flat major)

César Franck

Poco allegro

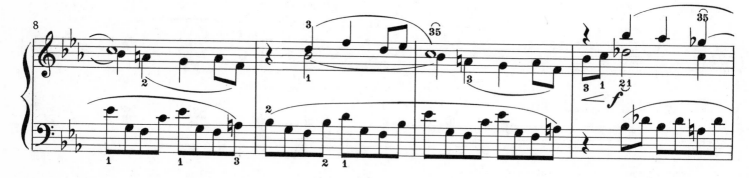

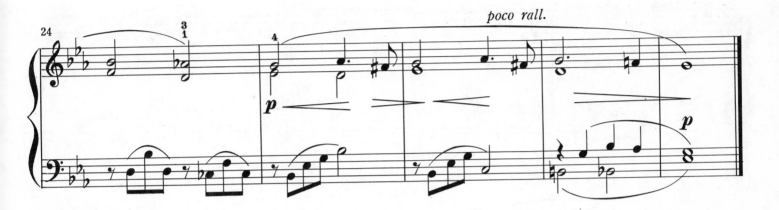

Cradle Song

Hugo Wolf

Longing For Home

Heimweh, Op.57, No.6

Edvard Grieg

Andante

poco rit.

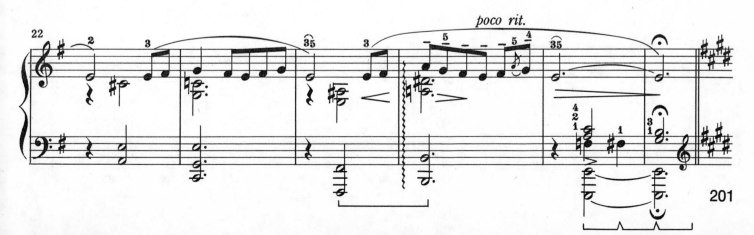

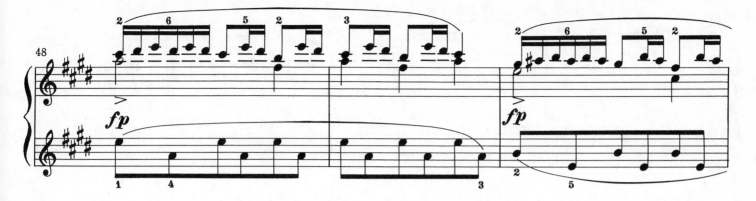

Tempo I

poco a poco più lento al Fine

rit.

Humoreske
Op. 6, No. 3

Edvard Grieg

Allegretto con grazia

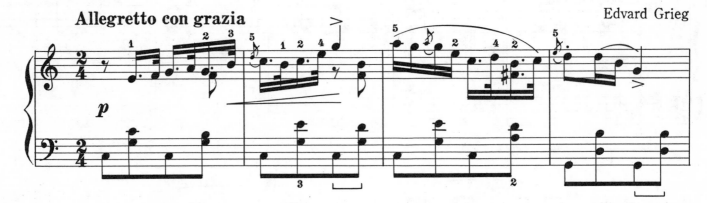

con fuoco

Notturno

Op.54, No.4

Andante

Edvard Grieg

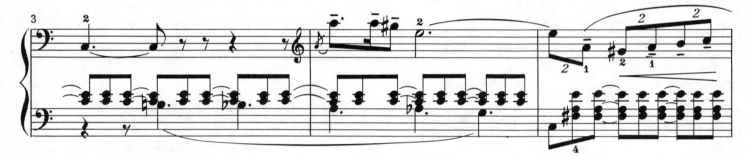

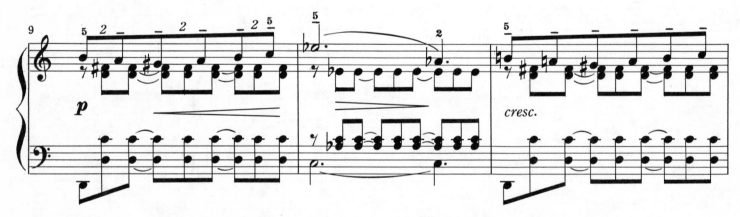

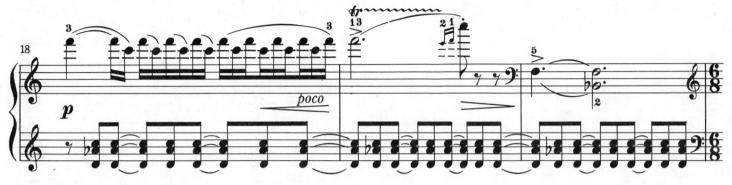

Più mosso

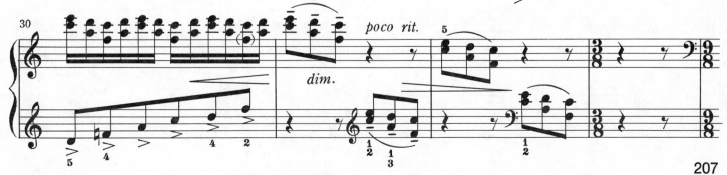

Tempo I

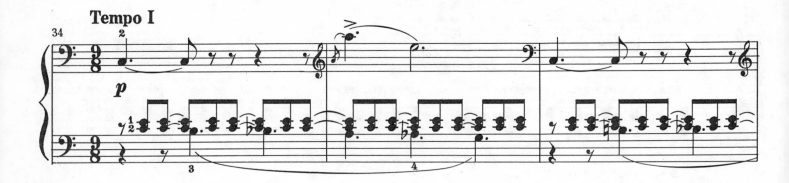

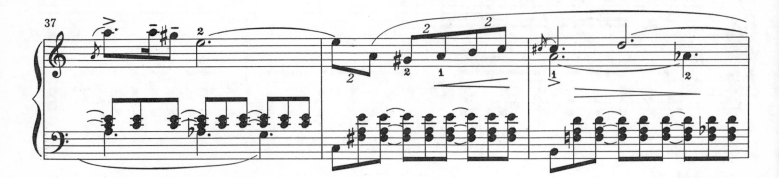

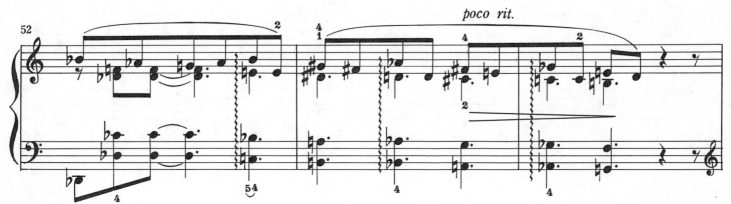

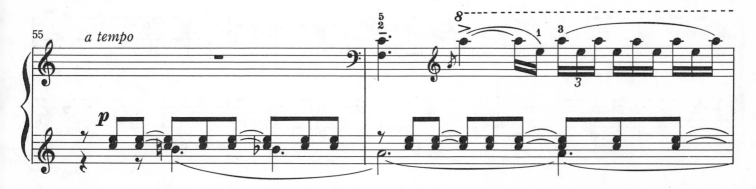

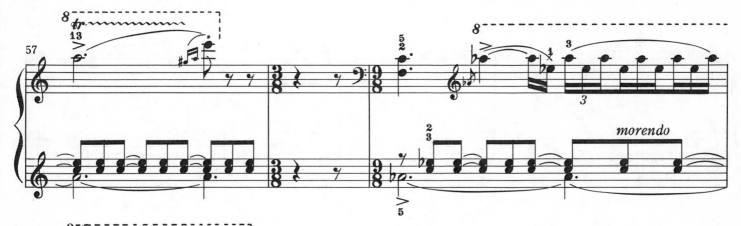

Puck

Op. 71, No. 3

Edvard Grieg

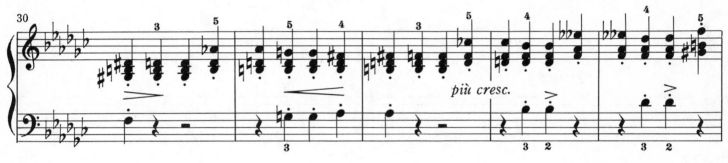

Serenade

Op. 3, No. 5

Serge Rachmaninoff

Tempo di Valse (*non troppo vivo*)

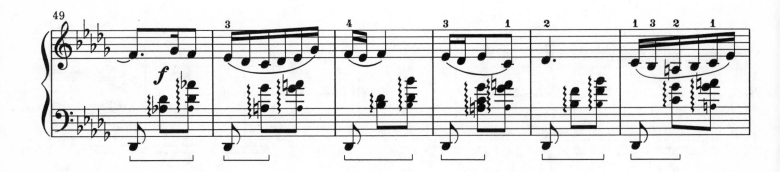

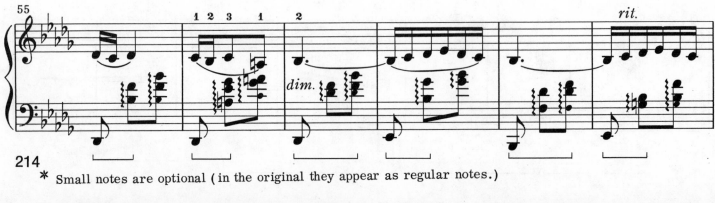

214

* Small notes are optional (in the original they appear as regular notes.)

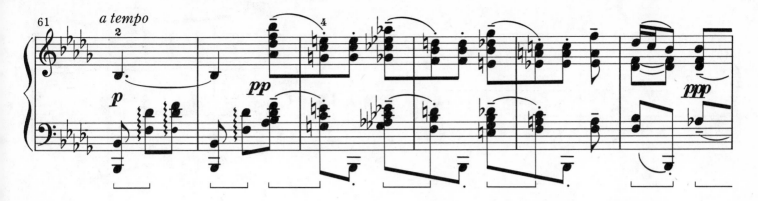

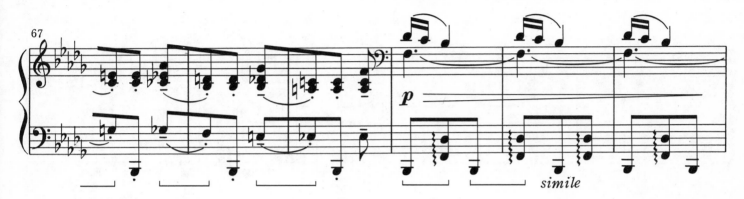

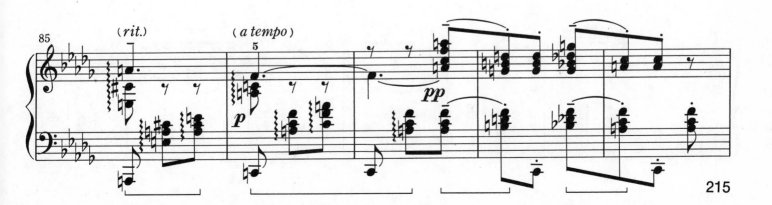

215

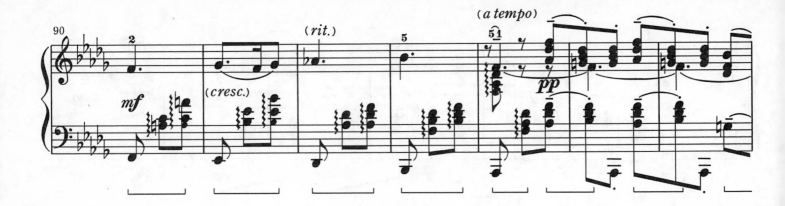

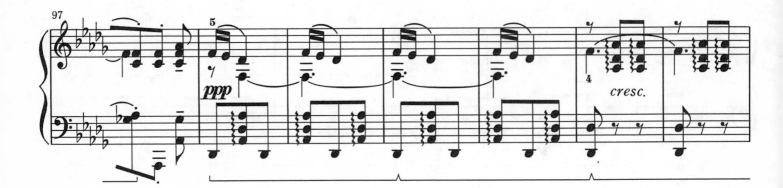

216

Moment Musical

Op. 16, No. 5

Serge Rachmaninoff

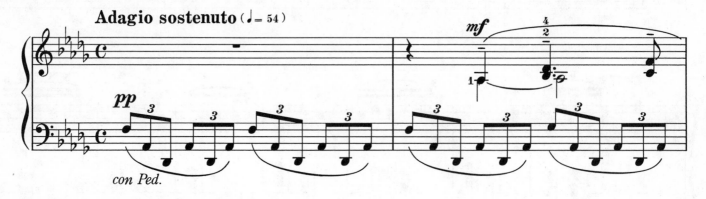

Capriccio

Op. 84, No. 1

Gabriel Fauré

Andante, quasi allegretto ♩ = 96

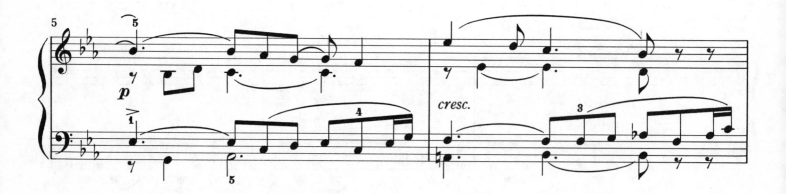

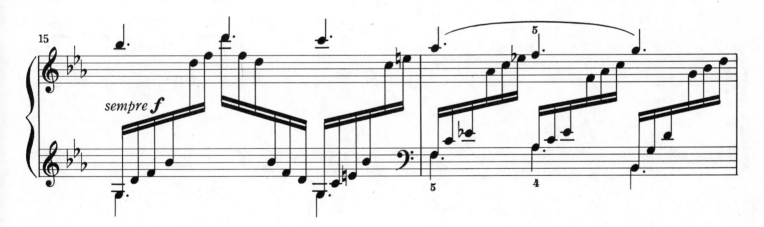

poco a poco crescendo

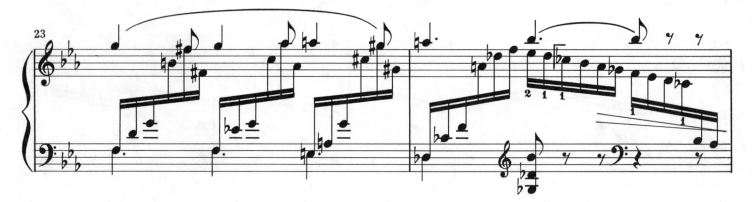

dolce

p

poco a poco cresc.

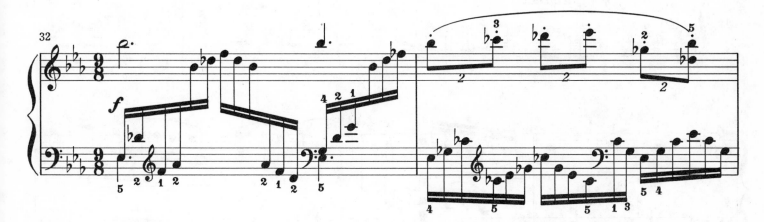

In Autumn

Op. 51 No. 4

Edward MacDowell

Buoyantly, almost exuberantly (♩. = 132)

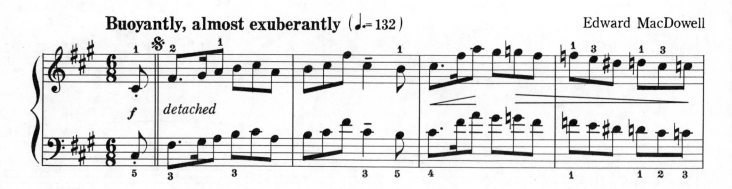

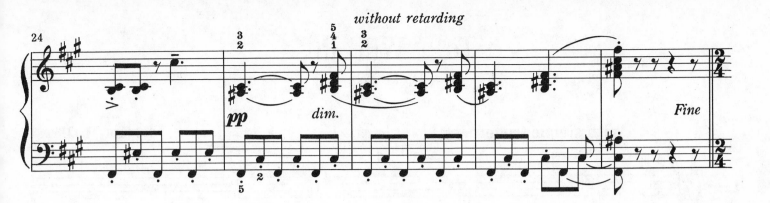

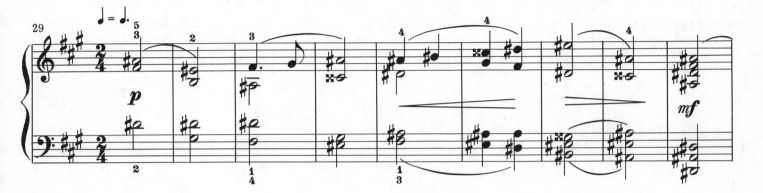

To a Wild Rose

Op. 51 No. 1

With simple tenderness (♩ = 88)

Edward MacDowell

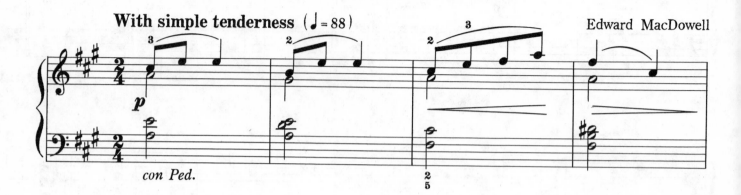

con Ped.

increase

still increase

slightly marked

228

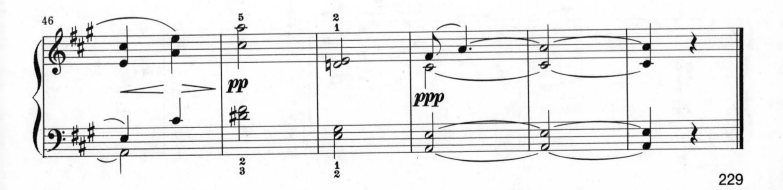

From Puritan Days

"In Nomine Domini," Op. 62, No. 8

Edward MacDowell

With measured emphasis (♩ = about 54)

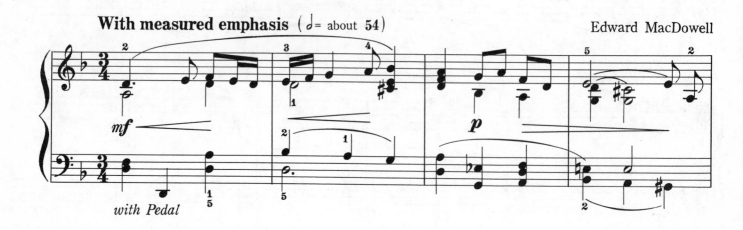

with Pedal

pleadingly

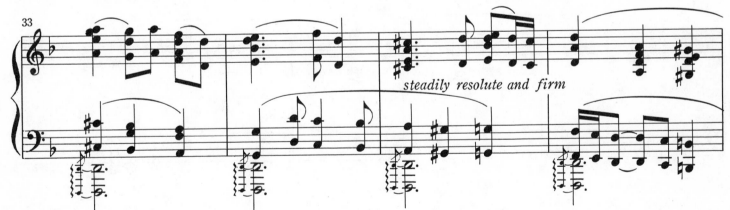

Pensée Melodique

Op. 40, No. 6

Con moto

Jean Sibelius

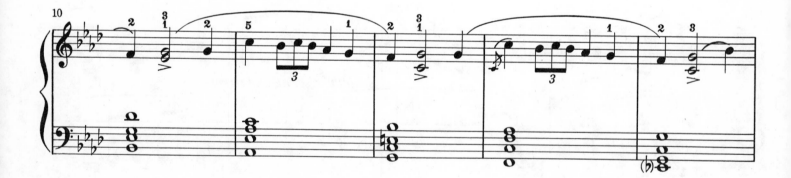

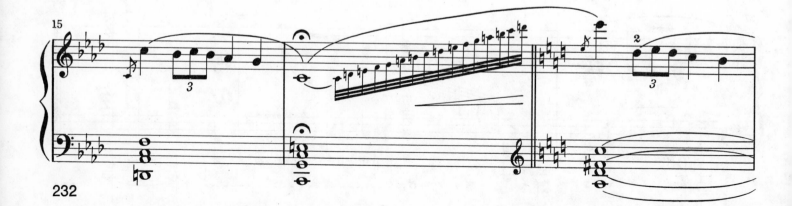

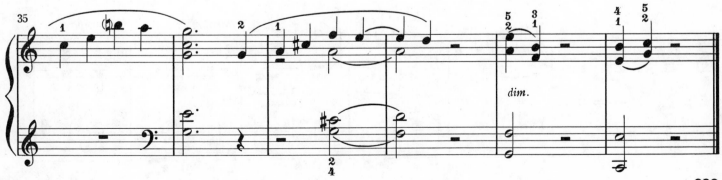

Zortzico

from "España," Op. 165, No. 6

Isaac Albeniz

235

Postludium

from "Winterreigen," Op.13

Ernö Dohnányi

Allegro non troppo

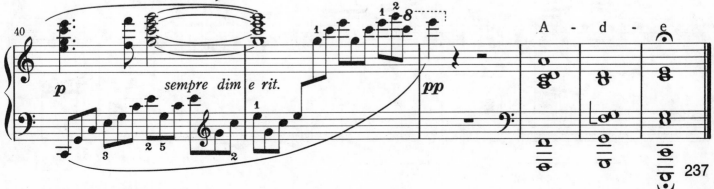

Burletta

Op. 44, No. 2

Very lively, with humor

Max Reger

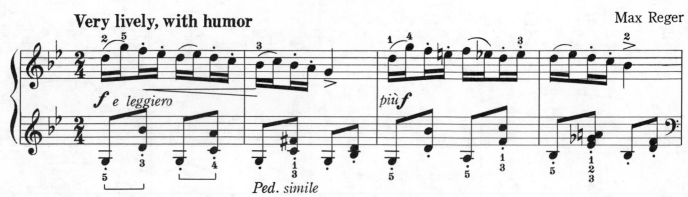

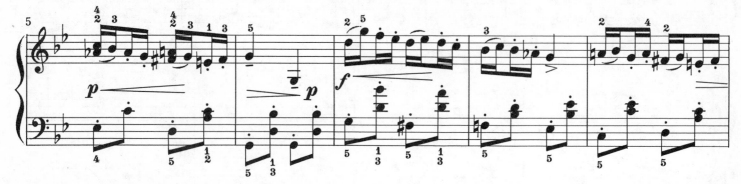

Album Leaf

Op. 44, No. 1

With expression, not too slow

Max Reger

BIOGRAPHICAL SKETCHES OF COMPOSERS

Albeniz, Isaac, b. 1860, Camprodon, Catalonia—d. 1909, Cambo-les-Bains, France. Spanish piano music, after languishing through most of the nineteenth century, came to life in a dazzling creative burst just before its close. An outpouring of folk-based compositions followed, led by works of Albeniz, Granados and de Falla. Albeniz fuses an intensely emotional, almost pictorial, musical sense with unbounded vitality and a technique for organization possibly gained by association, in France, with such figures as Fauré, Chausson, and Dukas. He is one of the most successful musical interpreters of his land and heritage.

Alkan, Charles-Valentin, b. 1813, Paris—d. 1888, Paris. French romanticist, a member of Parisian artistic circles which included Victor Hugo, George Sand, Chopin. His piano music is most effective and shows a great deal of harmonic originality. His works, almost completely ignored in his lifetime, have been performed with increased frequency in recent years.

Brahms, Johannes, b. 1833, Hamburg—d. 1897, Vienna. Hailed as successor to Beethoven; leader of opposition to the Wagnerian cult. Romanticist with classical predilections. Wrote much great music for piano; particularly characteristic are the intimate small pieces of his later years.

Chopin, Frederic, b. 1810, Zelazowa, Poland—d. 1849, Paris. Lured by Paris as a young man, he became, with Liszt, one of the dominant figures of the Parisian musical world. Composer of the most thoroughly pianistic music ever to appear.

Dohnányi, Ernö, b. 1877, Pozsony, Hungary (now Bratislava, Czechoslovakia)—d. 1960, New York. Eminent Hungarian composer, pianist. Taught at conservatories in Berlin and Budapest; played in principal cities of the world with great success; settled in the U.S. in 1949. Dohnányi's Brahmsian upbringing never stifles the exuberance of his Hungarian heritage. His piano music, though conservative for its time, has many of the virtues of both influences.

Dvořak, Antonin, b. 1841, Nelahozeves, Czechoslovakia—d. 1904, Prague. Best known of Czech composers. Reputation based largely on symphonic works, but composed some effective piano pieces. Spent several years in the U.S.—in Spillville, Iowa, a Czech community, and in New York as head of the National Conservatory.

Fauré, Gabriel, b. 1845, Pamiers, France—d. 1924, Paris. Piano music by Fauré is extensive, varied, and original. He combines a classical respect for clarity and economy with a very personal romanticism. The high esteem in which Fauré's music is held in France is gradually spreading elsewhere as his virtues, always subtle, make themselves felt.

Franck, César, b. 1822, Liége, Belgium—d. 1890, Paris. Belgian by birth, German by ancestry, and French by preference, Franck is one of the great figures of French music. Combines mysticism, lyrical qualities, and a Germanic solidity of structure, particularly contrapuntal skill. Had enormous influence on many younger French composers. His piano music is limited in quantity but uniformly high in originality and musical strength.

Gade, Niels Vilhelm, b. 1817, Copenhagen—d. 1890, Copenhagen. Most famous Danish composer, highly regarded by Schumann and Mendelssohn. His works represent an appealing blend of Mendelssohnian and Danish folk-influences.

Glinka, Mikhail Ivanovich, b. 1804, Novospasskoye, Russia—d. 1857, Berlin. "Father of Russian art music". Notable chiefly for his operas; left only a few, but characteristic piano pieces.

Grieg, Edvard, b. 1843, Bergen, Norway—d. 1907, Bergen. Foremost among composers writing in a nationalistic idiom. He absorbed his country's folk music to such extent that his own melodies are hardly distinguishable from the songs of his people. Most successful in the smaller forms, his individualistic harmonic thinking had great influence on young composers of the eighteen-nineties.

Heller, Stephen, b. 1814, Pest, Hungary—d. 1888, Paris. Friend of Schumann who valued his music highly. He was also closely acquainted with Chopin, Berlioz and Liszt. Wrote exclusively for the piano, mostly in small forms. His harmonic inventiveness and the intimate, poetic quality of his works assure him a special niche in the literature of romantic piano music.

Liszt, Franz, b. 1811, Raiding, Hungary—d. 1886, Bayreuth. Greatest piano virtuoso of the nineteenth century. As a champion of the Wagnerian musical ideal, exerted a powerful influence on European music. Generous in performing works of others, an unusual virtue in his day. Wrote much piano music in virtuoso style. A bold, important harmonic innovator of his era.

MacDowell, Edward, b. 1861, New York—d. 1908, New York. In the absence of serious competition in the late 1800s, MacDowell was hailed as the "Great American Composer". Thoroughly trained in Germany and imbued with the Beethoven-Brahms tradition, he did gain some international reputation. This tide has ebbed, however, and today we honor him for many delightful piano pieces which really show his considerable talent and stature better than his more pretentious works.

Mendelssohn (-Bartholdy), Felix, b. 1809, Hamburg—d. 1847, Leipzig. A leader and idol of musical Germany in the mid-nineteenth century. Famous as composer, pianist, conductor. Friend of Schumann. Wrote much piano music of romantic charm and classical clarity of form.

Moussorgsky, Modeste Petrovich, b. 1839, Karevo, Russia—d. 1881, St. Petersburg. Studied for a military career and his musical education was sketchy; still, through his unique intuitive and creative powers, he became one of the most original and most influential of all Russian composers. His works are deeply rooted in native soil and express a gamut of intense emotions from extreme tenderness to barbaric passion.

Rachmaninoff, Sergei, b. 1873, Oneg, Russia—d. 1943, Beverly Hills, California. A great pianist whose compositions combine a distillation of the Chopin-Liszt era with a strongly Russian personal expression. Often melancholy, sometimes violent, occasionally witty, the music of this most pianistic of Russian composers retains the most widespread popularity of anything written in our time.

Reger, Max, b. 1873, Brand, Germany—d. 1916, Leipzig. Highly original, widely respected German composer of neo-baroque and Brahmsian tendencies; also an acclaimed pianist, organist, conductor, and teacher. Many works in all categories are marked by late-romantic searching and restlessness, but also—especially in the smaller forms—by an appealing lyricism and occasional touches of earthly humor.

Schubert, Franz, b. 1797, Vienna—d. 1828, Vienna. The beloved composer of some of the best Western music, one of the great melodists of all time. Unequalled as composer of songs, he left as well much superlative piano music.

Schumann, Robert, b. 1810, Zwickau, Germany—d. 1856, Endenich. Leader of the young romantic "modernists" of the mid 1800's. Critic of highest integrity and lasting influence. One of the most original composers for piano; many revolutionary stylistic innovations. His wife, Clara, was his first important interpreter.

Sibelius, Jean, b. 1865, Tavastehus, Finland—d. 1957, near Helsingfors. Though chronologically displaced, a true romantic composer with strong Finnish nationalistic leanings. He is at his best in symphonic works, but a few pieces for piano show another side of his creative powers: an attractive, intimate lyricism.

Smetana, Bedřich, b. 1824, Litomsyl, Czechoslovakia—d. 1884, Prague. Great pioneering figure of a Czech nationalistic musical idiom. Was devoted to the preservation and exploitation of his country's folk music; immortalized the Polka as Chopin had the Mazurka.

Tchaikovsky, Peter Ilyich, b. 1840, Kamsko-Votinsk, Russia—d. 1893, St. Petersburg. Though piano music was a minor interest, obscured by his symphonic talents, a good many pieces remain to give us a sampling of this great Russian's infectious lyricism and beguiling melodic gift.

Volkmann, Robert (Friedrich), b. 1815, Lommatzsch, Germany—d. 1883, Budapest, Hungary. German composer who lived throughout most of his creative years in Budapest. Mendelssohnian lyricism, spontaneous, natural simplicity and joviality pervade the works of this, one of the most appealing of minor romanticists.

Wolf, Hugo, b. 1860, Windischgräz, Austria—d. 1903, Vienna. Almost all of Wolf's creative talent was devoted to the writing of songs, including many of the best in the literature. Among relatively few works in other categories is the charming piano miniature, "Cradle Song", of this volume.

GLOSSARY

Album Leaf A dedicatory musical thought to be entered in an autograph album. A short, simple piano piece of intimate character.

Barcarolle A romantic instrumental piece in swaying 6/8 time, suggesting the boat-songs of the Venetian gondoliers.

Burletta (Burlesca, Burla) Instrumental composition of jesting, farcical or grotesque nature.

Capriccio (Caprice) A lively, almost scherzo-like instrumental piece is the 19th century meaning of the term.

Consolations The title of six lyric pieces by Liszt, derived from and inspired by a volume of poems by the French poet and essayist Sainte-Beuve.

Davidsbündler Dances *Davidsbund* (The League of David) was an imaginary musical society formed by Schumann to dramatize his crusade against the shallow musical "Philistines" of his day. The members of the society were the *Davids-bündler*. The Davidsbündler Dances (op. 6) contain eighteen pieces. The initials E or F, placed after the individual dances stand for *Eusebius* and *Florestan*, fictional characters created by Schumann to symbolize his romantic dual personality. Eusebius is contemplative and dreamy; Florestan is impetuous and passionate.

Ecossaise Although the word means "Scottish" in French, this dance probably did not originate in Scotland, but was born in the ballrooms of Paris during the late 18th century. Similarly to the Contredanse and English Dance, it is in lively 2/4 time and usually consists of two eight-bar sections, each repeated.

Elegy A composition of plaintive or mournful character.

Etude An instrumental piece, usually built on a single figure or motive, designed to develop the player's technical ability. Some composers of the 19th and 20th centuries, especially Chopin, were able to combine the didactic purpose of this genre with a truly meaningful and often poetic musical substance.

Humoreske (Humoresque) A good-humored, capricious instrumental composition, usually in one movement.

Idyl A composition of lyric and pastoral nature.

Impromptu Character piece, usually written for piano by romantic composers. The term, "improvised" in French, suggests a certain spontaneous and extemporaneous quality. The finest examples of the genre are Schubert's and Chopin's.

Intermezzo In romantic piano literature the term designates a character piece of lyric spontaneity.

Ländler A country waltz of the Austrian, Bavarian, and Bohemian regions.

Mazurka Polish dance in 3/4 time. It is of moderate tempo, usually slower than the waltz, with accents on the second or third beat of the measure. Chopin's Mazurkas are the finest stylized examples of the genre.

Moment Musical A term, first used by Schubert, for a short, lyric piano composition.

Nocturne A "night piece"; lyric, instrumental composition of a quiet, reflective mood.

Novelette A lyric piano piece usually including a Trio. The term was first used by Schumann.

Pensée Melodique A "melodic thought", musical form similar to the *Moment Musical.*

Polka A lively dance in 2/4 time. It is probably of Czech origin and became extremely popular during the second half of the 19th century.

Polonaise Polish dance of a stately, processional character, in 3/4 time. It originated in the 16th century, probably from court ceremonies and it appears frequently among the works of 18th and 19th century masters. Chopin imbued the form with an intensely lyric, and often heroic substance.

Postludium (Postlude) An organ piece played at the end of the church service. Also, any brief, concluding composition.

Preludium (Prelude) Literally, a piece of music which serves as an introduction to another piece (such as fugue) or a group of pieces (as in the baroque suite). It is often written in a free form in the manner of an improvisation. Since Chopin, the title Prelude has been used for a short, independent composition, usually of a lyric, and sometimes of a descriptive character (Debussy).

Puck Grieg's title for his scherzo-like piano composition, after a character, a mischievous goblin, in Shakespeare's "Midsummer Night's Dream".

Rhapsody A Fantasy-like instrumental composition, usually in one movement, formed of loosely connected contrasting sections (Liszt's Hungarian Rhapsodies, Gershwin's Rhapsody in Blue). Brahms' Rhapsodies are more tightly organized, almost sonata-like constructions.

Romance A lyric composition of an expressive, intimate and tender character.

Scherzetto A little Scherzo.

Scherzino A little Scherzo.

Scherzo The Italian word for joke, jest. An instrumental piece of humorous, playful character in 3/4 or 3/8 time. It is usually the third movement of a sonata, symphony or string quartet and has the form structure of the Minuet, from which it evolved. (Pattern A—B—A, or Scherzo—Trio—Scherzo.)

Serenade (Serenata) Originally, evening music to be played under the window of the courted lady. The term came to denote a great variety of instrumental forms in one or several movements, for either a solo instrument or for various instrumental groups.

Songs Without Words (Lieder Ohne Worte) Mendelssohn's title for forty-eight piano pieces, song-like in form, mood and character.

Waltz (Valse, Walzer) The most popular dance of the 19th century and, in different stylized versions, a much cultivated instrumental form of romantic composers. Always in triple time, its tempo, mood and character can vary greatly.

Zortzico Spanish (Basque) folk dance in 5/8 time.